Quarterly Essay

CU00879745

CONTENTS

Quarterly Essay is published four times a year by Black Inc., an imprint of Schwartz Media Pty Ltd. Publisher: Morry Schwartz.

ISBN 978-1-86395-564-5 ISSN 1832-0953

Subscriptions – 1 year (4 issues): $49 within Australia incl. GST. Outside Australia $79.
2 years (8 issues): $95 within Australia incl. GST. Outside Australia $155.

Payment may be made by Mastercard or Visa, or by cheque made out to Schwartz Media. Payment includes postage and handling.

To subscribe, fill out and post the subscription card or form inside this issue, or subscribe online:

www.quarterlyessay.com
subscribe@blackincbooks.com
Phone: 61 3 9486 0288

Correspondence should be addressed to:

The Editor, Quarterly Essay
37–39 Langridge Street
Collingwood VIC 3066 Australia
Phone: 61 3 9486 0288 / Fax: 61 3 9486 0244
Email: quarterlyessay@blackincbooks.com

Editor: Chris Feik. Management: Sophy Williams, Jess Tran. Publicity: Elisabeth Young. Design: Guy Mirabella. Assistant Editor/Production Coordinator: Nikola Lusk. Typesetting: Duncan Blachford.

Printed by Griffin Press, Australia. The paper used to produce this book comes from wood grown in sustainable forests.

GREAT EXPECTATIONS

Government, Entitlement and an Angry Nation

Laura Tingle

Rome, October 2009. It was suddenly cold in the eternal city. Only a few weeks earlier I had taken a photo of our daughter, Tosca, standing in the heat of an Indian summer, smiling in her little girl's cotton shift, in front of the Pantheon.

At home, in the political world, the temperature had also suddenly changed. In fact, climate change itself meant that the beginning of the end of Malcolm Turnbull's leadership of the Liberal Party was looming, although not yet in sight. In a couple of months, the Copenhagen climate change conference would destroy Kevin Rudd's remaining hold on the climate debate and ultimately help to destroy his leadership of the Labor Party.

Tosca and I had escaped all this, leaving father and husband behind for an excellent girls' adventure in Italy. There had been hot, bright days in the countryside and among the ruins and Umbrella Pines. Now it was Saturday night in a chilly and wet Rome. Normally, we walked or caught buses around Rome, but our destination on this night – one of Rome's more distant hills – saw us competing for a taxi among the crowds at the end of Piazza Navona.

Abruptly we were seeing Rome as many tourists only see it: in terms of its hustling, excitable traffic. Tosca's fingers dug into my arm as we weaved wildly through cars that were all defining their own laneways through the wet streets.

Amanda Vanstone – former senator, former Howard government cabinet minister – was the Australian ambassador to Italy. I had known Vanstone when she was in Canberra and liked her. We weren't particularly close. She wasn't a great "fizz," as journalists like to describe good sources, but I had always marvelled at her capacity to survive the Howard era as one of the few Liberal "wets." He moved her in and out of cabinet, into all sorts of testing jobs. She did them without complaint, secretly relishing the times when she could get some policy shift past her boss. She always had a sharp and quirky eye for the workings of human nature. Now she was our representative in a country whose volatile and chaotic modern-day politics leave many Australians both perplexed and smug.

In response to an email asking if she could fit in a cup of tea, Amanda had extended a kind invitation to join her and her husband, Tony, for dinner. We talked of things Italian and Australian as the Vanstones' dog, Gus, lolloped about, refusing to live up to his reputation for biting guests. The Vanstones brought to the conversation both the detached clarity and intense interest of those who are living far from home.

We pondered the prospects of Malcolm Turnbull – perhaps the last hope of the small-l liberals – and we spoke of the much-maligned traffic after our hair-raising taxi ride across the city. To our surprise, we found ourselves agreeing that despite their reputation, Italian drivers were not as aggressive as those in Australia. Italian drivers looked for their opportunities. Everyone expected no less of everyone else. But they didn't deliberately speed up to cut you off as people do in Australia.

"Yes, but you see I've always thought Australians had an inbuilt angry streak," Vanstone observed.

Angry? All the clichés about Australia go to our easygoing natures. Happy-go-lucky, no worries, she'll be right. It had never occurred to me to think of Australians as an angry people. We might be moaners and whingers, but angry?

We think of the Mediterranean cultures as hot-blooded and hot-tempered, yet here we were in the centre of one of the oldest civilisations in the world, discussing how people on an everyday level got on with each other, manoeuvred around each other, so that everybody could get where they wanted to go.

We had just come out of a decade in which the country's political leader said he wanted us all to be "comfortable and relaxed," and, later, "alert but not alarmed." Yet Vanstone's comment stayed with me, perhaps because I was so regularly reminded of it even in the relatively sedate traffic of Canberra: so many people stubbornly refusing to give way when they could. Why should they let someone else get ahead? Australians might not like to yell and confront each other, we might not gesticulate colourfully, but we find other ways to assert ourselves.

This, of course, was before Tony Abbott's rise to the leadership of the Liberal Party, and before the June 2010 coup that toppled Rudd and injected a new level of anger into our political discourse.

Someone, it seems, is always in the process of letting us down or telling us a lie. No one in politics is allowed to change their mind, or even adapt to new circumstances, anymore. In the day-to-day political discourse, this is put down purely to bad politics, badly conducted. But are we also getting angrier as a society?

When I went back to Vanstone in late 2011 and asked her why Australians are so angry, she replied that it is because they have expectations that have not been met and a belief in entitlements they are due.

The more I thought on it, the more it seemed that so much of our culture, so many of our public discussions, contain some suspicion or assertion that we might be being ripped off, that someone else might be getting preferment. The belief that we are entitled to a lifestyle that we think everyone else may be enjoying seems to simmer not far beneath the surface.

A most conspicuous example of this is the way the debate about asylum seekers plays out: the swirling myths that people who arrive by boat are handed a goodie bag of entitlements as they step ashore.

The simmering suspicion is not a new phenomenon. But maybe it is a defining one that we are yet to acknowledge in ourselves. In his book *Convict Society and Its Enemies*, the historian John Hirst documents what he rightly says is perhaps "in all our writings" an un-bettered account of this aspect of Australian society. In 1839, during a heated debate on the future of convict transportation and self-government, a correspondent for the *Sydney Herald* wrote about the harshness of the relationships within the small but growing community. The *Herald*'s correspondent, who called himself simply "A Settler," pointed out that such harshness was in fact a characteristic of all new societies:

> People come here to better their condition, many with limited means, their tempers a little soured with privations and disap-pointed expectations (for all expect too much); cut off from the ties of kindred, old friendships and endearing associations, all struggling in the road of advancement, and no-one who reflects will be surprised that they jostle one another. Every man does not know his own position so well as at home.

*

Australia's politics and our public discourse have become noticeably angrier since that cold Roman night in October 2009. "Shouty," some people call it. And yes, the social media seem to amplify it and make it uglier. People think they can say just about anything to anyone in the semi-anonymous world of the Twitterverse.

In popular culture, some of the recent confected outrage may well have been imported as a package and a formula from elsewhere, notably the United States. In the political realm, we are underwhelmed by our politicians, by our institutions and by the quality of services that government provides.

But I want to explore something wider. This is not an essay that seeks to make grand claims about the Australian character or the Australian psyche. Neither is it another treatise pointing out the stunningly benign relativities of Australia's economic position and social harmony and that, as a result, we really don't have anything to complain about.

Rather I make the argument that as a nation, a polity, we have not sat down and worked out what exactly we expect "the government" – by which I mean its administrative side, as well as the politicians of the day – to be and to do. We haven't settled the idea of what we think we are "entitled" to get from government. The only things we seem to have been sure about over the years are that government has *not* met our great expectations that it will look after us, and that we are nonetheless entitled to be looked after.

Politicians may be the conduits who try to persuade us from time to time that they can make government work better. We talk endlessly of how they let us down, of how hopeless they are. I think this is only *partly* born of the fact that they may *actually* be hopeless. It is also – and this is much less discussed – born of the fact that we don't really know what we expect of them, or of government, in the first place. A friend of mine calls Australian politics "aorta politics": as in, "They oughta do something about it," even if what "they" oughta do is not clearly defined.

I will explore Australians' expectations and experience of government, and community and the state, and how they have changed over time. That is, what Australians expect the commonweal to provide for us, what we have come to believe we are entitled to, how this has translated into our political debate and how it has influenced politics in the past and the present. It is a slightly slippery topic, because it extends from the more immediate question of what we expect of our politicians through to notions of state paternalism and the reality of the services government delivers.

I am writing at a time when the people of some of the oldest Western civilisations on earth are being rudely forced to confront the question of just what they expect of the state. In Greece, a comfortable, creeping growth in the size of government has risen up to bite the citizenry. The shock being felt is not just over an argument about the need for budget restraint; it goes to the question of what constitutes the Greek state, its scope and its mission.

I also want to consider on the changing nature of what politicians and the polity can in reality do for us. At the heart of anger is disappointment or frustration. It is a disappointment at something expected, or hoped for, that has not been received. It is a frustration that things should be different. But what is it that we expect of government in Australia, and how have these expectations been formed?

The Australian commonweal has developed a little like the streets in Sydney's central business district. Down by Sydney Cove, the streets still essentially follow the goat tracks established by the first settlers. At the very time of an unprecedented revolution in Western thought about government and the rights of man, our nation started as an autocratic, bureaucratic penal administration, rather than a polity. We grew into a colony that perpetually wrestled with what a country at the other end of the world thought of us, trying to impress England with the idea that we were not barbarians but were more British than they were, while simultaneously growing proud of what we had established that was different and distinct.

We spent much of our first century with our politics focused on begging for favours or freedoms from a foreign parliament. Our colonial parliaments developed grudgingly, with incremental increases in control over our own affairs. And, of course, "stuff" just happened which pushed the economy and the population through waves of rapid change: the wool boom; the gold rushes; recessions and depressions; and, more than anything else, constant mass migration.

The colonies moved towards a federation travelling on ideals of unity and good for all. They even agreed to call the country a Commonwealth as this reflected an idea of the common good and the utopian and advanced way in which Australia seemed to be developing. Yet the actual constitution was constructed on the basis of economic interests rather than any great utopian ideas about the rights of man.

The services we enjoy receiving from government also developed in a piecemeal way. From the earliest days, Governor Arthur Phillip insisted that the children of the First Fleet's convicts should be educated. Phillip's pragmatic rationale was that education might stop the first generation of free-born white New South Welshmen following in the criminal foot-steps of their parents. It was not meant to rewrite the rulebooks for what government did, even though it meant, from the very start, that children born in a penal colony would gain an education that was not available to their contemporaries in the country from which their parents came.

Our school history lessons so often concern the idea of a confrontation between authority and the battling individual, between people claiming or asserting economic rights against an inflexible or unfair state – whether it be the Emancipists, the Squatters, the Rum Corps or the Eureka Stockade. These legends – along with that of the Diggers' scorn for hopeless English officers – have become part of the Australian cliché about our contempt for authority. They also reflect another cliché, about the Aussie battler doing it tough and being badly done by. But just as significantly, these legends are also reflections of the haphazard way in which our govern-ance developed.

Perhaps this is why, if you were to ask Australians, "not what your country can do for you, but what you can do for your country," most would respond with a blank look. We might believe that our country – our government – can do something for us, but, beyond military service, there is no deeply entrenched value ascribed to doing something for our country, or government. Public servants (who do generally have a commit-ment to the national good) are more often than not held in contempt, as are politicians.

Compare this with the United States where there is, confusingly, both a deep hostility to government, yet also a much more established tradition of civic service, whether it be in local, state or federal government or in the thousands of elected jobs for which Americans must run.

Government is rarely portrayed in any of our conversations as a force for good. More often it is seen as amorphous, badly run and ill-defined, the plaything of politicians that is separate from most of us. Similarly, Australians are dismissive and cynical about why people enter politics. We rarely discuss decisions in terms that recognise the compromises that government, and democracy, inevitably entails.

Our expectations of what government will do have seemed to grow over the years. Of course it will be there to assist us after bushfire or flood, not just with our immediate emergency needs but also by helping with rebuilding and providing income support. When we travel to war-torn and unstable countries, we expect government to rescue us from trouble, and, sometimes, to get us home.

We still expect government to intervene in industrial disputes that are causing the rest of us inconvenience, and to support workers left without their entitlements by collapsing businesses. We expect government to provide easily accessible hospital services, and good schools and childcare and roads and public transport. We expect it to protect little children when their families won't. We expect to be protected from violence and crime. We expect to be protected from our bad decisions about shonky investments made in the name of chasing a higher return.

Yet, at the same time, we see public anger that we have become a "nanny state." We see anger about tobacco and alcopops laws. There is anger when government tries to find a way of allocating water among millions of users that is sustainable and priced rationally.

This lies at the nub of the problem: our expectations and our sense of entitlement are confused and this makes us angry. Politicians spruik the virtues of small government, yet propose vastly expensive schemes without explaining how they will be funded. Politicians talk about fixing a problem like climate change, then opt for a policy that does little to address it. Politicians tell us we should be pleased we have escaped the global financial crisis, yet we complain that escaping it hasn't made it any easier to pay the mortgage or the electricity bill.

Our current "shouty" politics follow two momentous shifts in our relationship with government in the past couple of decades that have not been well understood. These are changes which have dominated my working life as a journalist and which I have observed up close. The first was the process of deregulating the Australian economy in the 1980s and the 1990s. The second came with the election of John Howard in 1996.

Paul Kelly defined the way we see the 1980s and 1990s in his seminal book *The End of Certainty*, in which he argued that the great era of deregulation dismantled the pillars of the Australian settlement that were implicitly or explicitly agreed at the time of federation: White Australia, industry protection, wage arbitration, state paternalism and imperial benevolence. Kelly argued that deregulation unleashed powerful new forces in Australia's politics, as well as its economy, which smashed this settlement. Writing as it was happening, his great achievement was to place the change in an historical perspective.

Yet there are things we can observe now which were not so apparent in the early 1990s. Kelly believed that the choice in politics would be between those who pursued this new Australia exposed to the demands of globalisation, and those who sought to retreat into the old world. But that is not quite how it has been turning out. What was not apparent then was that our politicians would not prove universally capable of leading us to understand the implications of dismantling the cosy "protection all round" world.

Our post-deregulation politics has been dominated by politicians reluctant to admit that one implication of opening up the economy is that they don't have quite as much control as they once did. In the old Australia, our economy contained institutions and policies that both protected us and gave our governments considerable control over events. Wages and work conditions were determined by a central body. Industries could be protected by tariffs and subsidies. The value of the dollar could be set by the government, as could interest rates. Such policies were the embodiment of a paternalistic world in which we had come to expect the state to look after us.

When the change came, there were some notable attempts at shifting people's expectations. Paul Keating famously warned in 1986 that if Australia did not reform its economy and adopt sensible economic policies, it would end up a third-rate "banana republic." His remarks prompted a 10 per cent fall in the value of the Australian dollar and galvanised a sense of crisis. Pollsters reported for the first time that people were talking about their collective responsibility to the economy. Bob Hawke and Keating seized the opportunity to push for reform that would better equip Australia for a competitive world.

They persuaded voters not only that they were not entitled to regular pay increases, but that they needed to accept pay cuts to help lower Australia's inflation rate. They persuaded voters that industry protection was a bad thing, although removing it would cost jobs. They argued that Australians could not presume that the state would fund their retirements through the age pension. The provision of an age pension had been entrenched early in Australia: the still very new federal parliament enacted legislation in 1908. By the 1980s it was regarded as an unquestionable right. To turn this expectation of entitlement around was difficult. But Hawke and Keating promoted the development of superannuation savings as a means of funding retirement, and in doing so pushed the revolutionary idea of self-sufficiency in old age.

Even amid all this, the Hawke–Keating governments used the levers at their disposal to protect Australians from the full force of change. Tax cuts were dispensed to make up for loss of wages. The "social wage" became part of a new national "settlement," offering free medical care, family income supplements for low-income earners, increased pensions and orderly transition plans for industry.

But just as Australians were being forced to alter – and scale down – their expectations of government for the first time in a century, John Howard made a U-turn and gave us the second big shift in as many decades. The promise was that we didn't have to change anything. Not only that – we were entitled to feel relaxed and comfortable. Howard's greatest political moments came when he persuaded Australians that they – and their government – were in control of events that they didn't feel in control of. His famous battle-cry about asylum seekers arriving by boat – "We will decide who comes to this country, and the circumstances in which they come" – remains the best encapsulation of this.

Howard – the supposed advocate of small government – built an entirely new edifice to service the expectation of entitlement. Australians were told that they were entitled not just to tax cuts, but to government support if they had babies, if they stayed in the workforce, if they took out private health insurance, if they bought a home. People who retired with their superannuation savings would never again have to pay tax, regardless of their circumstances. He limited direct government spending on education and health, but gave subsidies to those who used private education and health services. Howard gave us tax cuts as Hawke and Keating had done, but instead of using them to "buy" acceptance of change, soften its effects and achieve better economic outcomes for the nation, he used them as evidence of the Coalition's commitment to small government. In reality he was dressing up big government as personal entitlement.

There has been a third change, too, the one that Kevin Rudd tried to bring about but failed to deliver in full. After the complacency – and talk of less government – encouraged by Howard, Rudd rode to power on the back of a promise that he would transform the way government worked. Governments, he argued, could change the world. He argued that his could and would do something about climate change, while Howard had argued to the death knock that it could not. Rudd argued for a return to interventions that were made through direct government spending, rather than through individual entitlements. He wasn't just going to subsidise private health care, he was going to fix the hospitals. He wasn't just going to subsidise private schools, he was going to provide massive new funding for all schools.

Instead of telling Australians that they had to fend more for themselves in future, as Hawke and Keating had done, or that they were entitled to payouts from the government, as Howard had done, Rudd was changing the message about what governments could and should do. He was delving into the too-hard basket. He promised radical reform, but not reform that would hurt people, as the changes in the deregulatory 1980s had done; this was reform of institutions to make them work better for people.

Rudd told us that he could make our hospital system work better, and our schools. He identified the frustrations of voters with federal–state blame shifting, with the never-improving crisis that characterised our education system and hospitals. Voters had seen promises of more money for health and education doled out at each state and federal election without it materially changing anything.

The vast ambition of Rudd's agenda, the fact that it – at least briefly – changed once again the expectations of the role of government, has been lost in the ensuing failures to deliver and in the change of circumstance that came with the global financial crisis. Instead we've seen a return to deep cynicism about our politicians and what it is that governments can do, and do well.

*

It is not just the changes in political message that have led to our growing confusion. It is not just that politicians don't like admitting that they don't have the means to change things. It is also that the pervasive presence of politicians in the media has forced them to take on an even bigger role in public discussion, even as they have less power to influence events. In a relentless 24-hour media cycle, politicians are the ultimate free providers of content. They are always on hand to comment on anything that might be going – from something that actually does concern them in the political world through to the latest sporting win or controversy.

It used to be the case that questions asked at question time in federal parliament were directed to the responsible minister, not to the prime minister. Ministers spoke only on matters within their portfolio. That restraint has been lost in recent years. With the increased demand on politicians to have something to say on every topic, it is little wonder that many rely on stock lines provided by the prime minister's office each morning. Or that prime ministers overshadow their governments.

While the role of politicians has been changing, so too have the institutions we deal with every day, as the pendulum has swung from public sector to private. The institutions we rely on to deliver services and run our community were once arms of the state. Now these necessities are delivered by the private sector. Transport, banking, electricity, water, insurance and telecommunications: all these sectors were once wholly owned or else heavily shaped by major publicly owned institutions operating in their markets. Even in the fields of health and education, the rise of the private sector and the relative decline of the public sector has been occurring apace in the last few decades. As a result, we have become increasingly angry about corporations and their influence over our lives, but we also still hold government responsible for the shortcomings of markets that they no longer control.

Twenty or thirty years ago, the image of a group of council workers having a smoko, not working, by the side of the road, was a wonderfully simple metaphor not just for inefficient government, but for our lackadaisical approach to life. Whom do we complain of now? Private institutions, such as banks and telecommunications companies and their outsourced call centres.

Our view of politics has failed to keep up with the implications of this shift from public to private. Deregulation, obviously, involves government ceding control over large parts of the economy, whether it be the rate of interest banks can charge on mortgages, the value of the dollar or the wage-setting process. The politician who once had ultimate control over the person who installed your phone, or who ran the local jail as an employer and manager, has become simply another shareholder, or a contractor of services with much less say, and less clear lines of account-ability, than their predecessor thirty years ago. The terms of our political debate are still framed by the expectation that governments can control events, or at least protect the community from them. But because our leaders seem as powerless to control private sector institutions as we are, we are constantly reminded of their impotence – and we don't like it.

In the early 1980s, federal ministers still controlled the interest rates on housing loans. Then these were deregulated, the Reserve Bank was made more independent, and banks moved interest rates up and down in a reflection of the RBA's money-market cash rate. Politicians would emerge to take implicit credit when interest rates moved in the right direction, or to explain why it wasn't their fault if they didn't. The fact that their actions had little to do with the result was irrelevant.

More recently, with banks borrowing more and more of their funds offshore, the banks have argued that the domestic cash rate is not neces-sarily an accurate reflection of their cost of funds. So they have started not to move their home-loan rate when the official rate moves. This should be the ultimate test of market forces: if customers don't like what their bank has done, they can move to another bank. Instead, the political argument becomes one of whether the treasurer of the day has enough machismo to bully the banks into doing what he or his critics want.

Language about the size of government also spiralled out of control in the last few decades. Politicians no longer talk at elections or budget time about how much they will spend in a year, but about how much they will spend in four years. The amounts spent on health and education in an expanding economy therefore always seem to increase. In fact, in the Howard years, as a percentage of GDP, health and education spending declined significantly, as money was transferred to security and defence, to counter-terrorism and waging wars. Popular frustration and confusion about failures in health and education resulted. Coming on top of the loss of control that was still flowing from the deregulatory period, it was no wonder that Australians became confused about exactly what it was governments were supposed to do.

Politicians set expectations. They are also the conduit through which people's expectations about the state flow. But expectations also build up insidiously over time. We may not know why the givens of any particular policy debate are given. They seep in quietly over the years until someone comes along to challenge the entire edifice that has built up without our realising it.

A person's sense of entitlement in life – what they expect their life to look like – is all-pervading. A person may have a small sense of entitlement, or a large one. It will shape their sense of how capable they are of changing their life – should they wish to change it – or of creating the life they desire.

I noted earlier that we don't value our politicians or public service. Yet our leaders have often risen to the challenges laid down for them. In the 1890s, we created a social and economic compact built on a huge wave of prosperity. Whatever the constitution's limited ambit at the time of federation, you have to wonder whether our present generation of politicians could achieve anything close to this. Is that because the politicians then had to argue only among themselves – state to state – and not against a whole new layer of federal representatives and bureaucrats?

We struggle today to find either a politician or a message that can give effective, inspiring voice to our personal or national aspirations. We fight attempts at intervention that aim to fix our problems, such as the mining tax (yet complain about the impact of the high Australian dollar) or a carbon price (despite wanting politicians to do something about climate change just five years ago).

Much of the debate about the nature of Australian politics, and about our policy settings, naturally refers back to federation, since that was when "Australia" got started. But the structures, and perhaps more importantly the habits and expectations, of much of our governance were established, and had become entrenched, well before that.

Amazing things were happening in the world when Arthur Phillip and the First Fleet left that world in May 1787 and made their way to Australia.

A congress of American colonies had published a Declaration of Independence from England a decade earlier, stating that "all men are created equal" and had "certain unalienable Rights," including Life, Liberty and the pursuit of Happiness. No one had put things quite like that before. Declarations dating back to the ancient world and up to the beginnings of the English parliament had set out what might be expected of the rulers of a particular society, or where the people might fit into that society, but no one had ventured to start from the basis of an individual's rights and on that foundation fashion a political order.

The world, and the world of ideas, was being turned on its head in the wake of the Age of Reason. In France, the state's financial instability was provoking resistance among the nobility to the imposition of taxes, and a public clash with Louis XVI. There was civil unrest in the Dutch Republic, the Netherlands and Poland.

As the First Fleeters were spending their first months at Sydney Cove, the American colonies were, one by one, ratifying the new constitution of the United States. In the newly formed union, George Washington took office as the first president. The Americans had, by a series of deliberate and deliberative processes, created a nation suffused with the ideas of the Enlightenment.

Eighteen months after Phillip arrived at Botany Bay, the French Revolution would burst forth with the storming of the Bastille. The French had begun a process that would eventually, and painfully, overturn the old order across Europe.

It is hard for us to comprehend just what huge changes these were, how they overturned all the rules, from the most basic statements of human rights to the seemingly most trivial considerations.

In his book on the second American president, *John Adams*, David

McCullough documents the heated discussions among the American founding fathers about what to call the president of their new republic. Should they call him "Your Highness"? The US Senate took a month on the question of titles, which superseded all other business. A committee appointed to consider the issue reported back with the suggested title, "His Highness the President of the United States of America and Protector of the Rights of the Same."

George Washington, in the meantime, had sent out a list of queries to trusted confidants about appropriate presidential behaviour. Would it tend to "prompt impertinent applications and involve disagreeable consequences," he asked, "to have it known that the President will, every morning at eight o'clock, be at leisure to give audience to persons who may have business with him?" After all, that was how things were done in the royal courts of Europe. Despite the Americans having just fought a long war to throw off the British monarchy, this was the only model they had for the protocols and expectations of government. Etiquette and titles were questions of form, not substance. But to those self-consciously trying to create something new, they were worth getting right.

On the other side of the world, Arthur Phillip was also establishing a new society. It was not one bothered by revolutionary ideas or the conundrums they created. But that is not to say Phillip lacked ambition. "What Frobisher, Raleigh, Delaware, and Gates did for America, that we are this day met to do for Australia, but under happier auspices," he reportedly told his motley crew after his commission as governor of the new colony was read on 7 February 1788.

> Our enterprise was wisely conceived, deliberately devised, and efficiently organised, the Sovereign, the Parliament, and the people united to give it their authority, sanction, and encouragement. We are here to take possession of this fifth division of the globe on behalf of the British people, and to found a State which, we hope, will not only occupy and rule this great country, but will also be

the beneficent patroness of the entire southern hemisphere. How
grand is the prospect which lies before this youthful nation!

With his allusions to British explorers and fortune-seekers in the
Americas, Phillip's ideal was one of imperial grandeur. Little thought had
been given to how the penal colony might function over time as a society
or a polity; instead it would develop in a happenstance way. Isolation
would create some wildly contradictory pressures on the nascent polity. It
had no parliament or delusions of democracy, and no imported social
structure. Thanks to King George III's lofty supposition of *Terra Nullius* it
had no land ownership issues to consider. Eddie Mabo and the High Court
were 204 years in the future.

Phillip's colony contained neither a governing class nor a group of
land-owners. It comprised a governor with autocratic powers, his administration, such as it was – military officers doing things in a military
fashion – and a labour force, which hardly saw itself as part of a commonweal. The First Fleet marine Watkin Tench described in his journal
what we may call the new colony's first institutions of government. The
bureaucracy of the governor and commander-in-chief included a judge
of the Admiralty Court and judge advocate of the settlement, a surveyor-
general and a commissary of stores and provisions. There was also the
military establishment – the ships of the fleet and four companies of
marines.

In the absence of the institutions of their home society, Phillip – and
his successors up to Lachlan Macquarie – made up the rules by which the
colony worked, not only for the convicts, who were their direct charges,
but also for the increasing numbers of emancipists and, later, free immigrants. These were rules of justice and land entitlement, working hours
and individual freedoms. The governor and his establishment ran everything and provided everything in the colony. Being at the mercy of the
governor, and ultimately of the English monarch, put all the groups of the
new community on a similar footing.

These days the popular view of our earliest society remains one of downtrodden convicts being lashed and manacled in chain gangs under the control of tyrannical soldier guards. Yet the picture painted by historian John Hirst is much more complex. Hirst argues that perceptions of the colony of New South Wales were heavily influenced by its role as a pawn in political battles of ideas in Britain, including those fought on the abolition of slavery and prison reform. The colonists spent a good deal of the time and effort they dedicated to politics challenging these perceptions abroad – because they had such an influence on their rights and the future of the colony – rather than thinking about where they were headed at home. The political debates that mattered were the ones that took place in Westminster, and they were reported, belatedly, at length in the Australian papers.

The advocates of abolition in England went to some lengths to portray the colony as a slave society. It is true that convict labour was forced labour: conditions were harsh in penal colonies such as Port Arthur and Norfolk Island. But for the majority of the convicts, in Sydney, their experience was built much more on the power relationships that flowed from an unquenchable demand for labour. "The masters of New South Wales had to struggle hard to get these people to work at all and it was they who forced the masters to settle for something much less than having good servants," Hirst notes in *Convict Society and Its Enemies*. Even in the first couple of years of the colony, when it faced starvation, most of the convicts did not assist by working the land properly:

> They seemed totally irresponsible; they would rather consume rations from the store and live in idleness than work in the fields, and yet without more crops the store would soon be exhausted … This madness of a penal colony at the Antipodes was not of the convicts' choosing. They could reckon that before Phillip and the officers would allow themselves or the convicts to starve something would be done. As indeed it was – the *Sirius* was sent to the Cape of

Good Hope for supplies; to reduce the number of mouths to be fed some of the convicts were sent to Norfolk Island; fishing parties were instituted; the *Supply* sailed for Batavia. Not if they could help it, would the convicts be the settlers of Australia.

The power of labour to set its terms, right back in those earliest days, saw official hours of employment set down, then rapidly restructured to account for the fact that overseers couldn't keep convicts at their work all day. Convicts were allowed to earn private income when not at their government labours, so they had a particular incentive to get away from these as fast as possible. The basis of payment quickly became taskwork – finishing a job – rather than hours worked. Equally, convicts felt enough power to insist on being fed wheat rather than maize. Even on Norfolk Island, convicts refused to eat the potatoes they were given. These developments show how a significant part of the population quickly made pragmatic judgments about governance: what it would provide, and what they in turn must do, or not do, for themselves.

Like so much of what happened in the new colony, the adoption of taskwork as the basis for pay – which would entrench a series of presumptions about labour and its rights – happened without any planning. But like a lot of the other rights the colonists gradually acquired, it also happened without much of a fight.

The early malaise of the penal colony began to be transformed – socially and economically – by a class of enterprising emancipated convicts, who saw the opportunities open to them in a country where all the land and all the influence had not already been claimed. As we have seen, there was education for their children. The convicts, emancipists and eventually free immigrants also found themselves with rights they would not have possessed in England. An employer could not arbitrarily flog a convict worker (such things had to be approved by a court). Tench has described that convicts had the legal right to sue for damages, ignoring English laws under which convicts were unable to be witnesses, to bring actions or to own property. The press, as it developed, was freer than in England. The early twentieth-century historian Marion Phillips, in her book *A Colonial Autocracy*, described the colony's military government as a curious and anomalous system of autocracy working through the forms of civil law.

*

So "Australia" started as an uncommon mixture of absolute power in government, held by a governor acting for an absent ruler, and pragmatic arrangements reached, and powers claimed, by a population that carried the negotiating clout of rare labour in a place where there was so much to be done. It wasn't until Lachlan Macquarie arrived as governor in 1810 that the colony found itself under an autocrat (the last) who made a concerted effort to create some serious, permanent infrastructure and to look with fresh eyes at a society that was no longer just a penal settlement.

Macquarie restructured the administration and better organised some local sources of revenue that could supplement the funding from England. There were duties on the coal and timber trade from Newcastle, liquor licences and court fines, cattle-slaughtering dues, as well as the net profits of goods sold through the public store. The money from a police fund was used to build a jail, wharves, bridges and roads, and to pay a growing group of public servants. An orphan fund paid for the various charity schools. In a more creative form of private–public partnership, the governor allowed three businessmen to build a hospital, partly out of the profits of a rum monopoly. He also oversaw the establishment of a proper local currency. Within a few years of Macquarie's departure, the colony would be financially self-sufficient.

Macquarie, like his predecessors, governed with doubtful constitutional authority, and by the time he arrived, the governor's position was under pressure both in the colony, where the locals were demanding a representative and accountable system of government, and in England, where the raison d'être of the penal settlement was being questioned.

Despite restoring order and bringing considerable improvement to the colony, Macquarie was perhaps the first leader about whom Australians grizzled for doing both too much and too little. Having dispensed with the unpleasantness of the Rum Corps rebellion, he found himself in a society where tensions between the emancipists and others had built to the point of real conflict. Twenty-two years after the arrival of Phillip and the First Fleet, people were trying desperately to establish a social pecking order, a class system of their very own. This was a task made difficult by the fact that such a large proportion of the populace were emancipists – and wealthy emancipists, what's more – whom both the military and free immigrants sought to exclude from "society." To Macquarie's credit he recognised the very different nature of this society and that people accustomed to the social order of England would need to adapt to one where wealthy didn't necessarily mean of gentle stock and ex-convict didn't mean social outcast. He invited former convicts to functions at Government House. Politically, he backed the cause of emancipist lawyers against the military and judicial establishment.

In 1819, the explorer, and later politician, William Charles Wentworth wrote his *Statistical, Historical, and Political Description of New South Wales*, with the ostensible aim of attracting potential settlers to the colony, instead of other prospects such as the United States and Canada. However, Wentworth, the son of a convict mother and a father with connections to the aristocracy at a time when lineage was important, also had a bigger cause in mind. Wentworth's father, D'Arcy, was a central figure in Macquarie's administration, and the son goes out of his way to praise the governor's contributions ("Never was there a more humane and upright man"). He fumes nonetheless that:

> dignified feeling cannot exist in any society which is subject to the arbitrary will of an individual; and although the governor of this colony does not exactly possess the unlimited authority of an eastern despot, since he may be ultimately made accountable to his sovereign and the laws, for the abuse of the power delegated to him, I

may be allowed to ask, should he invade the property, and violate the personal liberty of those whom he ought to govern with justice and impartiality, where are the oppressed to seek for retribution?

He alludes to "outrages" carried out by governors, "of which the bare recital would fill the minds of a British jury with the liveliest sentiments of compassion and sympathy for the oppressed." Wentworth called for the colony to have its own elected assembly with wide powers. Emancipists should be allowed to vote, he argued, but the right to vote should be based on property holdings. He wanted trial by jury, no taxation without parliamentary approval and free migration. Such reforms would help the colony rise "from the abject state of poverty, slavery, and degradation, to which she is so fast sinking, and to present her a constitution, which may gradually conduct her to freedom, prosperity, and happiness."

The importance of 1819 is that it marks the beginning of years of incremental change in our governance, questions of its legitimacy, and dissatisfaction with our leaders and politicians. The Bigge Commission of Inquiry, initiated in the same year, led to the 1823 *New South Wales Act* passing through parliament in England. The Act changed the central and autocratic power of the governor by establishing a legislative council, proper court system and the capacity to challenge the governor's decisions. It also heralded a change in the way the colony perceived itself, and was perceived elsewhere, and saw the emergence of political leaders and advocates.

Over the next twenty years, the governor's powers were gradually eroded further, as "non-official" members of the legislative council were appointed, representing landed and wealthy interests. Simultaneously the colony started passing its own laws on everything from how the postal system worked to how money was collected for various services, and how government officials behaved. Many of our institutions became firmly entrenched, such as tax collectors, the police force, hospitals and schools.

The development of a polity was an incremental, piecemeal process.

Transportation of convicts to New South Wales effectively ended in 1840. Around this time there was a push for male suffrage based on property holdings. But this was opposed by free immigrants, because the property law not only *didn't* keep former convicts from voting – many of them had now become wealthy land-owners – but also excluded poorer free immigrants. The battle became largely irrelevant, however, with the gold rush, which began in 1851. Consequent inflation made the property qualification, which had been set on English prices, worthless. The rush also had as large a transformative effect on the population as anything that had come before it – and with no rules set down by governors or nascent parliaments to stop it.

In 1858, an *Electoral Reform Act* abolished the property requirement and gave the right to vote – and to vote in secret – to almost every adult male in New South Wales. This included most workers, such as the miners who had flocked to the colonies for the gold rush. The franchise became wide by accident and, as a result, there was a change in the nature of our politicians that set the scene for a long history of contempt.

The rapid move to democracy, Hirst argues in *The Strange Birth of Colonial Democracy*, saw the rich find it hard to get elected and they "were forced to retreat to the upper houses":

> Poor men of little education replaced them. Members heaped vulgar abuse on each other and some were only in parliament to benefit themselves.
>
> Parliamentarians still dressed as gentlemen and hoped to be treated as gentlemen, but now there was an implosion: no-one believed that parliamentarians were gentlemen ...
>
> Rich and educated people now regarded politicians as a low class bunch of incompetents. They made fun of those who could not speak or write properly, who had done lowly work before they became MPs and who had wives who could never be accepted into good society. If a rich and well-educated man did get into parliament,

he was always apologizing for keeping such low company. It did give him a lot of good stories to shock and amuse his friends.

These very ordinary politicians had been elected by the votes of ordinary people. Their votes gave them the opportunity to show that they did not want parliamentarians to be just the rich and the well-educated. They elected parliamentarians who could not look down on them and whom they did not have to look up to. But they had not got rid of the idea that parliament was a place they should be able to respect. By their votes they had produced parliaments that they too despised.

Does this sound familiar?

There are individual politicians in our history whom we have come to respect, or at least regard affectionately. But Hirst shows us that the roots of our longstanding contempt for politicians is not just part of a recent worldwide trend:

> A vicious cycle had set in. Parliament was despised, but voters continued to elect men who kept its reputation low.
>
> In recent years, it is said, the reputation of politicians has fallen. If this is true, the change has been very small compared to the catastrophic collapse that can be dated precisely to the introduction of democracy in the 1850s ...
>
> So these are the inauspicious beginnings: a democracy ashamed to speak its name run by politicians who are held in contempt.

The speed with which we became a democracy was dazzling. It occurred over decades rather than centuries, given the absence of long-held titles to land that in England had brought with them instant entrées to political power and influence. We gloried in our prosperity and good fortune. We glorified our economic gain and physical hard work. But we fought relatively little for rights, since so many of these came as part of our British inheritance. The sort of rights that would be fought for, such as those that led to the establishment of the labour movement towards the end of the nineteenth century, occurred after many of our democratic structures had been settled.

During the 1850s, gold exports suddenly exceeded the wool trade, which had shaped the economic development of the colonies up until that time. As the former Reserve Bank deputy governor Ric Battellino noted in a February 2010 speech, at its peak in 1852 gold mining comprised 35 per cent of GDP (compared with less than 6 per cent for mining today). "This created tremendous upheavals in the economy at the time ... Labour flowed strongly to the gold states, particularly Victoria, and Melbourne became the largest city in Australia," he said. The population shifts were extraordinary. Immigration trebled the national population in ten years. Yet the demand for labour meant wages still rose sharply: between 1850 and 1853, wages in Victoria rose 250 per cent.

The massive expansion of the population increased the demands on young colonial governments for services. The colonies were not sufficiently large to produce individuals wealthy enough to build infrastructure, so it was up to governments to provide roads and, later, railways – at a time when the physical expansion of the country was at its height. Governments became big employers, particularly during the downturns of an economy that shifted violently between growth and contraction with changes in the international demand for wool and gold. Men would commonly march on government buildings demanding work when things were difficult, and politicians would oblige. At the same time, the colonial governments passed legislation to provide free, compulsory and secular elementary education for all children at schools operated by the state, abolishing state funding to the many schools that had been established by religious groups. All this was accomplished without the need for income taxes. While there were import duties and liquor licences, the really big source of revenue was land, and the sale of land seemed to provide an almost unending source of funds.

The next decades saw the rise of the labour movement and the push for federation, the point at which most people start examining federal politics.

But the problem with starting a survey of our politics, governance and institutions in 1901 is that we overlook how much of our governance was already entrenched, which federation would not change. The way we viewed our politicians had been set. White male suffrage had been established, and white women in some colonies had begun to get voting rights. The bureaucracies that delivered many of our government services had been installed. Many of the laws that determined how we lived, our rights, even our rail gauges, had been passed. A strong expectation that governments would ultimately look after us and provide us with work had firmly taken root, along with our cynicism about politicians.

Mark Twain visited Australia in 1896. His wonderful and sharp observations of Sydney society show how the once all-powerful role of the governor had been hollowed out, yet how we still clung to what he represented – government and authority – as the centre of our world.

> If you enter your name on the Visitor's Book at Government House you will receive an invitation to the next ball that takes place there, if nothing can be proven against you.
>
> And it will be very pleasant; for you will see everybody except the Governor, and add a number of acquaintances and several friends to your list. The Governor will be in England. He always is. The continent has four or five governors, and I do not know how many it takes to govern the outlying archipelago; but anyway you will not see them. When they are appointed they come out from England and get inaugurated, and give a ball, and help pray for rain, and get aboard ship and go back home. And so the Lieutenant-Governor has to do all the work. I was in Australasia three months and a half, and saw only one Governor. The others were at home.
>
> The Australasian Governor would not be so restless, perhaps, if he had a war, or a veto, or something like that to call for his reserve-energies, but he hasn't. There isn't any war, and there isn't any veto in his hands. And so there is really little or nothing doing

in his line. The country governs itself, and prefers to do it; and is so strenuous about it and so jealous of its independence that it grows restive if even the Imperial Government at home proposes to help; and so the Imperial veto, while a fact, is yet mainly a name.

Thus the Governor's functions are much more limited than are a Governor's functions with us. And therefore more fatiguing. He is the apparent head of the State, he is the real head of Society. He represents culture, refinement, elevated sentiment, polite life, religion; and by his example he propagates these, and they spread and flourish and bear good fruit. He creates the fashion, and leads it. His ball is the ball of balls, and his countenance makes the horse-race thrive.

He is usually a lord, and this is well; for his position compels him to lead an expensive life, and an English lord is generally well equipped for that.

The debate about federation was conducted in this curious world that Twain visited, framed by colonies suddenly looking offshore with some sense of stability and prosperity, for whom the governors had largely become an irrelevance in terms of politics, despite still representing the heights of power and influence.

The move to federation would be driven by economic considerations (protection versus free trade) and by fear of the world outside (keeping Asians out, developing a viable defence force). The debates leading to federation saw powerful ideas of state intervention – reflecting what were already our great expectations – become enshrined in the new national government: conciliation and arbitration between employers and their workforce; White Australia; protection. But the actual settlement of powers for this new government, the constitution, contained little in the way of grand notions of what the nation might become.

In a display cabinet in the foyer of the federal Treasury in Canberra, there is a ledger, written in fine copperplate, the work of the first secretary to the Treasury, George Allen. As if for a small business, the book contains the new Commonwealth's day-to-day expenses in 1901: items such as, "delivery of luggage of Members of Parliament expense, about one pound per week, may be charged to the vote of 10,000 pounds for conveyance of Members of Parliament."

Allen headed one of just seven departments foreshadowed in the federal constitution, the others being those of the Attorney-General, Customs, Defence, External Affairs, Home Affairs and Postmaster-General. Allen, a man without formal qualifications, started work with just five staff. As Treasury grew, Allen also became commissioner for pensions. In 1910, he established the Land Tax Office to service the new federal taxes.

They didn't have political fetishes about budget surpluses in those days. Yet the federal government's revenue in the first 1901–02 budget was estimated at £10.3 million, while Commonwealth spending was estimated at just £3.7 million. The Commonwealth was required under the constitution to pass surplus revenue back to the states. "Of the tariff receipts," Treasury records in its official history, "the major item (£2,975,374) was in respect of stimulants (alcoholic drinks) and narcotics (tobacco and opium products)."

The point of all this? We forget that the federation started with modest ambitions for the federal government and with the states jealously holding on to as many powers as they could.

The federal government's differing ambitions for domestic and international affairs can be measured by the fact of its finances being managed in a ledger, as against the sweeping arrogance of one of the first laws passed by the new parliament. Prime Minister Edmund Barton introduced the Immigration Restriction Bill – the legislative basis for the White Australia policy – to federal parliament on 7 August 1901 with a certain sanctimonious grandeur, quoting from Charles Benson's *National Life and Character*. "We are guarding the last part of the world in which the higher races can live and increase freely for the higher civilization," he intoned. "I place before the house a measure of definite and high policy."

Like the history of incremental shifts in power to the NSW colonists in the early years of the nineteenth century, the history of the federation – particularly the financial history – reveals a piecemeal increase in the federal government's duties and powers. Commonwealth pensions were introduced in 1909, a land tax in 1910, and the first Commonwealth coins were issued only in 1911. An "entertainment tax" was introduced in 1917. Two world wars made a difference, of course. Commonwealth income taxes were introduced as a temporary war measure in 1915 and reintroduced permanently during World War II. Arrangements for funding education, health, disabilities and roads all developed in a similarly piecemeal fashion.

Federation was the first point at which the country could design a future for itself. The most heatedly negotiated issues concerned government intervention: free trade versus protection, centralised wage fixing. The issues that helped to maintain the drive to federation as these battles raged were external and defensive ones: the desire to keep Asians out and fears that we were vulnerable to invasion.

In a speech in 2005, the Labor senator John Faulkner reflected on Henry Parkes' call in 1889 for the colonies to work towards federation:

> Twelve years later, Australia became a nation. I find it hard to imagine Australians today having enough faith in our political classes to bring the Commonwealth Government into existence. But then, Henry Parkes was not asking his contemporaries for that much faith. His appeal was for a government of limited powers compared to our government today, and by insisting on a directly democratic model, Parkes' model of federalism extended the power of the Australian people rather than the power of Australian politicians.

The founding fathers had strictly defined and limited aspirations for the new federation, but seeping through its fabric was a history of not just government intervention but also high expectations of what government would provide. Paul Kelly writes that:

> The nation was founded not in war, revolution or national assertion, but by practical men striving for income, justice, employment and security ...
>
> Australia was founded on: faith in government authority; belief in egalitarianism; a method of judicial determination in centralised wage fixation; protection of its industry and its jobs; dependence upon a great power (first Britain, then America), for its security and its finance; and, above all, hostility to its geographical location, exhibited in fear of external domination and internal contamination from the peoples of the Asia/Pacific. Its bedrock ideology was protection; its solution, a Fortress Australia, guaranteed as part of an impregnable Empire spanning the globe.

Much of what was constructed through the federation – not the constitution itself, but the agreed policy framework that saw the colonies vote in favour of change – would be undone in the 1980s and the 1990s. Centralised wage arbitration eventually came to an end, as did the edifice of industry protection. As to the White Australia policy and imperial benevolence, they had already started to unwind, but some might argue we have never banished them in sentiment. However, the pillar of the Australian settlement relevant to this essay is the one that we don't hear quite so much about, and which is perhaps the least understood: faith in government authority, or state paternalism.

Kelly defines it as "individual happiness through government intervention" and notes its origins in 1788. "The individual looked first to the state as his protector, only secondly to himself," he writes, going on to quote the earlier history of Keith Hancock, who wrote in 1930 that "to the Australian, the State means collective power at the service of individualistic 'rights.'

Therefore he sees no opposition between his individualism and his reliance upon government." And Donald Horne noted in *The Lucky Country*, "the general Australian belief is that it's the government's job to see that everyone gets a fair go."

The idea of state paternalism is embedded in our relationship with government, and has been since the time our convict forefathers expected Governor Phillip to fix the small problem of starvation rather than do anything about it themselves. We have expected governments to intervene to create equality. The very way funding is divided up among the states is based on a premise that everyone in Australia, no matter where they live, is entitled to a similar level of government services. More than the other pillars, it is an implicit idea, buried in policy and politics – not explicitly stated in the way that the commitment to a working wage or to the ANZUS alliance have been.

Perhaps for this reason, state paternalism has never been dismantled, or even identified and exposed to analysis, in the way the other parts of the settlement were. The capacity of governments to intervene on our behalf, to protect us, was obviously reduced by the dismantling of the '80s and '90s, yet we have largely ploughed on, expecting governments to act as they did in a world where they had many levers of economic control, which have now disappeared.

And in the failure to break down the habits of state paternalism we have the seeds of much of our modern national anger. We have had many arguments about the explicit policies. We have had debates about deregulating particular industries, and about the need for smaller government and less taxation. But we have never debated what the implications of deregulation and a smaller state might be for our expectations of government itself. Do we Australians understand that government no longer has the control of things it once did? Do we understand that the corollary of less tax is less ability to fund services? Are we comfortable and relaxed with that idea? What will we put in its place?

The great political battles of the 1980s and 1990s were fought over the idea that government intervention in markets was bad and removing it was good. But the implicit belief that government would ultimately put things right has proved the hardest to shift, perhaps because it is so intrinsically tied up with the business of politics. Politicians are always telling us what they can do for us, or what they have done for us. We, in turn, always expect politicians to fix things we aren't happy about. Our history has been one of politicians looking for opportunities to intervene, to protect us from the harsh realities of the world. State paternalism is what politicians do. It is a hard habit to break.

Yet the old habits came under enormous pressure from the time the Hawke government floated the dollar in 1983. No one had predicted the float or promised it as part of a political manifesto. It was set off simply enough by newly powerful financial markets putting irresistible pressure on the exchange rate following the election of a Labor government, which, to the markets, had overtones of a return to the financial chaos and excessive spending of the Whitlam years.

The push to undo the Australian settlement – for that was what the floating of the dollar triggered – was politically bipartisan. Pressure for reform had been resisted for decades, with the renovation of many economic institutions and structures long overdue. The states had continued to regulate large sections of the economy, meaning there were no uniform rules for doing business across the country. The highly regulated financial system could not provide flexible finance to underpin economic growth. Few argued that we shouldn't deregulate the economy (and those few that did were howled down); most debate was about the speed with which it happened and how to protect people through the change.

Previously, if you brought money into Australia as an investor, it was hard to get it out again. Now money could come and go as international investors saw opportunities and assessed how competitive we were with other countries. This meant we had to improve the systems of governance over our corporate sector, give companies access to the finance they needed to restructure, and make them stand on their own two feet.

Yet here is the crucial point: voters weren't consulted about the changes – except belatedly at the ballot box, when both major parties were in fundamental accord. There were few negotiations with the states. The government and its major spokesmen – Bob Hawke and Paul Keating – became both teachers and proselytisers to the Australian community about the need for a new economy. They did this from a defensive position, for there was suddenly a new constituency to win over: the financial markets. The markets brought suspicion, and sometimes hostility, to their view of a Labor government. Hawke and Keating found themselves not only trying to explain the benefits of deregulating markets to the electorate in political lingo that everyone could understand, but also having to deal with constant demands to prove their bona fides to sceptical bankers, brokers and international financiers.

These were alarming times to live through for a populace that had been protected from the ways of the economic world. The currency became a floating measure of our net worth. When the Australian dollar went up or down, so did the polling for the government. The electronic media started giving the daily value of the currency at the end of their bulletins, along with the sports results. We were being hourly valued by the rest of the world, and, it often seemed, not very highly.

Most dramatic was the "banana republic" crisis of 1986, which saw the value of the dollar plummet and an alarm ring out about foreign debt and foreign investment. This crisis galvanised the public debate. The prime minister addressed the nation on Sunday night prime-time television. There was a high-profile "Buy Australia" campaign, complete with sentimental theme song. The polls at the time suggested that while voters didn't like this new uncertainty – so far removed from the relatively safe world they had lived in until this point – they were persuaded that Australia needed to change.

Leading the economic education of the Australian populace was the treasurer, Paul Keating. Before Keating, economic debate had played a limited part in political discussion, only raising its head at times of crisis, such as the regular recessions that had dogged Australia. There might be a debate about high inflation or high unemployment, but as often as not it was seen as a reflection of something the rest of the world was also experiencing. Debates about government budgets were also limited, although there were exceptions: Whitlam's spending binge, and the legend of Malcolm Fraser's "razor gang" (which turned out to be more of a threat than a reality). Now the whole story of how government spending, taxing and borrowing interacted with the economy was up for discussion. In Keating, the community had an eloquent, entertaining and persuasive schoolmaster.

"Current account deficits" became a topic of general interest. Keating popularised all sorts of esoteric concepts, such as the J-curve – the idea that Australia had to import a lot of capital goods in the short term to boost its output and exports and that, as a result, the current account would get worse before it got better. Cartoonists even drew J-curves in tabloid newspapers.

Keating's lectures worked, and they gave the electorate some ownership of the reform process. Labor's pollster Rod Cameron recorded the mood at the time and remembers "finding ordinary people in the suburbs being at least at the first level of understanding economics and the need for deregulation. They would use words like that. This was an extraordinary revelation to us."

The idea that Australians were living beyond their means came to the fore and the public started to contemplate what it might mean for them and for the country. Cameron says that:

> The secret to Keating's educative skill was that he was not just able to lecture, he was able to bring it home to the kitchen table. And it became something that people could buy. Australians will respond to something like that. They will say, look, as long as I can see that it is going to be good for future generations, or my kids, I will cop some pain. They won't always do this, but there is a chance that

they will buy that message if you can explain how it will help future generations.

Australians endured this period of reform because they were persuaded that it would produce better outcomes for their kids, for the future. The government might have been undoing the structures that had helped establish the cosy world of state paternalism, but it was also promising voters that the change would leave them in a safer place in the long term.

The political debate was not taking place at the level of what the reforms might mean for the individual, or what citizens could expect of governments in the future; it was being fought at the level of institutions, such as the centralised wage-fixing system, and the national economy. Between the conflicting demands of the Australian electorate and the markets, the government tried to forge a new path, a new relationship between the individual and the state with which to secure the people's support for a new economy.

The government also challenged the major lobby and interest groups to debate issues in terms of the national interest, rather than their own interests narrowly conceived. It was the era of "peak body" summits. The Accord struck between the government and the trade union movement during the 1980s and early 1990s harnessed the centralised wage system to buy the deals that helped Australia make the economic transition. The Accord bought wage restraint and, as a result, lower inflation. In return there were individual tax cuts, targeted welfare assistance and increased superannuation. There was also the "social wage" – all the elements of state paternalism repackaged: an implicit contract that, in return for wage restraint, there would be new services and help from the government.

While on the one hand seeking to protect people from the ravages of change, the Hawke–Keating government also tried to make clear to voters that they could no longer presume that the state would look after them as it once had. The state would provide enough funding to universities to ensure places for those wishing to attend, but students would now have to make a contribution once they saw the financial benefits of their education. Workers would now be expected to negotiate directly with employers on an "enterprise" basis rather than through relatively anonymous, industry-wide negotiations. They would be expected to make concessions about their conditions in return for pay rises, all aimed at boosting the productivity of the business. But there would be a "safety net," a non-negotiable floor under pay and conditions across the economy, to ensure workers were not exploited. People would have to start paying more for their utilities – phone, water, gas and electricity – to reflect the market cost of providing them, but they were promised that competitive markets would keep these costs down. Perhaps most powerfully, there was a debate about retirement incomes. Following a review of the social security system, the message went out: Australians could no longer presume that the state would finance their retirement through an age pension.

Until that point, superannuation had been an expensive financial product, with limited appeal to lower income workers with cash-flow problems. It was sometimes a tax break for those who could afford it. Companies that provided super schemes sometimes saw them as no more than a mildly dodgy source of captive investment in their own shares. Few people took it seriously as a source of funds for retirement. In fact, a notable feature of the superannuation system was the "double dip." This was the process by which you retired, spent your super on, say, an overseas trip or a boat or a caravan, then went on the pension. In an age when it was not fashionable to defend the indefensible, I have a clear memory of a Labor backbencher coming out in defence of the double dip on behalf of her constituents. They've saved for their retirement, she argued, so they are entitled to spend their super however they want *and* they are entitled to the pension because they've worked and paid taxes all their lives.

In the 1970s, during Malcolm Fraser's prime ministership, politicians and newspaper headlines had trumpeted the need for crackdowns on dole cheats. But these discussions had always been about taking welfare away from people who "didn't deserve it," and cutting excessive spending (implicitly, excessive spending initiated by the Whitlam government). But now it wasn't just the dole cheats losing unfairly gained benefits. Most Australians saw things such as the tax concessions provided to super-annuation, or even the age pension, not as welfare but as rights. The idea that welfare should be available on the strict basis of need was new. Every-one would have to start expecting less of government.

And then came the recession of the 1990s. Hundreds of thousands of jobs were shed from both the previously protected parts of the economy, such as the car industry and the textiles, clothing and footwear industries, as well as the large range of federal and state government utilities: electric-ity generators, the telecommunications monopoly and transport systems. Adding up the job losses in 1991, I documented up to 114,000 jobs that had gone in the previous couple of years and another 220,000 that were earmarked to go.

Not only was government no longer protecting jobs, it was also aiding and abetting in cutting them. Some people lost their savings as financial institutions went to the wall. Governments didn't always intervene to save the institutions or reimburse the customers. Others lost their shirts in the speculative push into equity markets, fed by a newly deregulated access to credit and debt. Housing prices fell as inflation subsided. The great Australian obsession with property had one of its rare sour moments. We saw the downside of deregulation, of opening up our economy and the withdrawal of government, in one frightening period of uncertainty.

The spectre of the recession magnified the unfolding human drama of competing ambition between Hawke and Keating, and the emergence of an unrestrained free-market agenda from a Coalition led by John Hewson. The government broke under the strain and re-created itself under a remade Keating. He left the front bench as the man who had preached the need for fiscal discipline and micro-economic reform. He returned as a Keynesian intervener. Paul Keating, prime minister, advocated government spending to kickstart the economy and a big outlay on roads and rail. Big tax cuts were promised once again – although for the first time these were not a trade-off but simply a move to match those offered by Hewson. Keating also spent more time trying to define Labor's social goals in an era of economic change. His social messages were not directed at the general population but at specific groups. Whether it be for indigenous Australians or the unemployed, Keating's message was that as a nation we should "reach back" for the poor and dispossessed and ensure people were not left behind.

But having carried voters with him so far along the path of economic change, he didn't seem to recognise that the recession had left them feeling exposed and vulnerable. And, of course, the faith that had developed that Keating knew what he was doing was shattered. In 1993 Keating (the change merchant) won an election by promising to be the bulwark against more – and more radical – change. The push towards radical free-market economics within the Coalition came to an abrupt halt with the defeat of Hewson's Fightback! proposals at the 1993 election. The Coalition conceded it had gone too far for the electorate's liking and spent the next couple of years softening, sometimes disowning, Fightback!

With Keating changing the story, and radical reform defeated, the language of politics and its subjects of interest changed dramatically after the 1993 election. Voters had grown tired of accepting that deregulation and change would be good for the economy, and therefore good for them. They wanted to hear once again that government was there to make things better. Politicians stopped talking so much about the economy and reform, and started talking of other things. The Accord, and the social wage that had accompanied it as the basis of a new "settlement" defined by Labor, ran out of steam.

By 1996, voters were even more tired of rolling change and tough medicine. They were tired of Keating's prime ministerial calls for social change, too, whether it be on Aboriginal land rights or the republic. Keating would be defeated in that year by John Howard, who promised voters some respite and, in the process, redefined the relationship between government and voter. Howard offered empathy to Australians and told them they were "battlers." He wanted Australians to be "comfortable and relaxed" and brought us back to the idea of state paternalism, even though so much had changed from 1983 onwards in a way that could not be unchanged. He promised to protect voters from the new migration threat: boat people. He ramped up our relationship with the United States when the world became scary. While Labor had offered tax cuts and social services as part of a clear compact on wages and agreement to reform, Howard simply told voters that they were entitled to government support.

In a speech in 1995, Howard diagnosed problems in the relationship between government and individual as "due [in part] to the perceived inability of governments to solve basic challenges and to cure the many social ills, and arrest the processes of disintegration which have overtaken so much of Western life in past decades." People had lost faith in government. He noted a "world-wide shift to the right in the policy debate on economic issues," which, coupled with the end of the Cold War, had resulted in a "less ideological political debate." This, in turn, had led to a "de-tribalisation of politics," and, with uncommitted and swinging voters becoming more numerous, "election campaigns themselves have assumed much greater significance."

Howard's analysis of how the political debate had changed did not directly address the biggest change of all: the impact of economic deregulation on expectations of government. However, he sought to reassure voters that he and the Coalition were moving away from the hard-line economic arguments of the past:

> I have never seen economic rationalism, economic efficiency – or call it what you will – as an end in itself or a stand-alone political credo ... Australian Liberals are not blindly hostile to government but they are profoundly suspicious about what governments can achieve and are concerned about the concentration of power now in the hands of government. For Liberals the role of government should always be strategic and limited ... A proper balance must be struck between a healthy scepticism about what governments can achieve, and the

Australian tradition of believing that there is a role for government
which goes beyond it being a mere keeper of the ring.

Howard's speech acknowledged both the "Australian tradition" of a
wider role for government, and the Coalition's preference for a smaller
role. He spoke of smaller government in the sense of "getting government off people's back," but promised that the Coalition would not be
going to the extremes espoused by leaders such as Margaret Thatcher and
Ronald Reagan.

In fact, his 1996 election platform was not about small government as
much as a small target. There was a plan to sell off part of Telstra to finance
an environmental fund, but both the partial sale and the environmental
pay-off were acknowledgments that privatisation was one of the few
deregulation issues that voters would regularly baulk at, from the 1990s
to the present day. There were reforms to unfair dismissal laws as an aid
to small business. Howard also adopted Labor reforms like Medicare – a
big economic intervention that the Coalition had furiously opposed for
years – as a core value.

Howard offered a retreat from reform and change and a shift to talking
about the desires of individual Australians. In the wake of the Hewson
years, he recommitted to terms such as a "decent social security net," "a
strong health system" and "expanding educational opportunities." After
years of national crisis and real cuts in wages to break the back of inflation, Howard said he aimed at "restoring a sense of progress, where our
children are better off than we are, that once again our standard of living
will be among the highest in the world."

With his resounding victory, Howard came to office arguing that the
Hawke and Keating years had seen Australian politics dominated by a
small group of vested interests, notably the trade unions and "elites," and
promised to give government back to the community. In doing so, he
rewrote the history of the 1980s. He recast the intent of peak-body politics
from what it had been – an attempt to reach agreement on national goals

– to something dark and sinister. He claimed authorship of financial and industrial deregulation, but quietly walked away from many of the changes that had taken place with his support. He shifted the political debate from one about changing institutions for the betterment of the economy in the future to one about personal empathy with voters.

Howard inherited an economy that had shaken off recession and its aftermath. With a floating exchange rate and low inflation, the nation could finally defy the boom–bust rhythm that had shaped so much of our history. His government's first budget cut government spending hard: labour-market programs, the states, the public service, universities, nursing-home residents, the unemployed – all were targeted. Howard also imposed new taxes. It was not an exercise he would ever repeat. But, combined with a resurgent economy, it was sufficient to set the government up to return to surplus.

The Coalition's story about the economy became a very simple one about reducing government debt. This embraced both the politics of Labor as an untrustworthy economic manager and a fear of outsiders taking control of the country. The idea that we were losing control of our national sovereignty because of our high levels of debt had been a key message of the Coalition's 1996 election campaign, and it reflected a fear that was to find voice on talkback radio and in the politics of Pauline Hanson.

By the time Howard came to office, the headline economic reform issues of the 1980s had largely been addressed. Long time-frames for cutting tariffs, for example, had been set in place by the Hawke and Keating governments and rarely had to be revisited. When the car industry's tariff phase-down came up for review during the Howard years, the prime minister instituted a pause.

Howard and his treasurer, Peter Costello, stopped talking about the economy in the way Keating had, stopped having the monthly press conferences to explain what was happening. Yet, after attacking Labor for years for not reining in foreign debt, Howard presided over an increase in it at a time when Australia's terms of trade were the best they had been for a generation. A country's foreign debt funds the cost of the difference between what it exports and what it imports. Even if governments cut their debt by not spending as much, someone still has to borrow overseas to cover the difference. Under Howard, however unwittingly, it was households that started to raise foreign debt via their demands for credit from banks that borrowed overseas on their behalf.

Rod Tiffen and Ross Gittins point out in the 2009 edition of their book *How Australia Compares* that Australian household debt in relation to disposable income almost doubled during the Howard years. Some other countries have even higher levels of household indebtedness, but Australia is now considerably above the average. A central reason for this was the increasing price of housing, with Australia experiencing one of the sharpest rises in prices worldwide, so that mortgages in relation to income grew prodigiously during the Howard years. This suggested increased financial stress for many people, despite the relatively good economic growth.

But, as Tiffen and Gittins also observe, current account balances, household debt and house prices were outcomes of markets. Government had limited influence over the decisions of the individuals and companies who traded in those markets. They continue:

> At first the Howard government thought that rising home prices
> was good news: "I haven't found anybody stopping me in the
> streets, shaking their fists and saying John, I'm angry that the value
> of my house has gone up," said Howard during the first years of the
> housing boom, a tone that would change later as housing afforda-
> bility became a vexed political issue.

Howard's response to the increasingly difficult politics of housing was to offer subsidies for first-home buyers (which only inflated prices further) and general tax cuts, and to blame the states for a lack of developed land leading to higher prices.

An important part of his political formula was the "Howard battlers," the large group of traditional Labor voters who moved to the Coalition in

1996. John Howard's political strategy for the next eleven years had them as its central focus. In reviving and redefining the idea of the battler, Howard began a process of reinforcing voters' notions of how tough they had it. Not that the hardship was the fault of the government, mind you, but it was always on the lookout for how it could help. Having noted the de-tribalisation of politics in the 1980s, Howard moved to create his own tribe. The battlers were not just low-income earners, but middle-income earners too. In fact, it sometimes seemed that few people couldn't be classed as battlers. Government became a source of endless avuncular tax cuts and new cash entitlements: the baby bonus, the first-home owner's scheme, the private health insurance rebate. There were no more messages about having to fend for yourself at retirement. Of course, the government spoke in favour of every person's right to make decisions without government interference. It was just that, whatever you did in life, there seemed to be a government payment to help you along the way.

Talk of reform faded after the big spending cuts of the 1996 budget, with the exception of the introduction of the GST four years later. As for small government, that was well and truly forgotten. A paper produced by the Treasury noted that the growth in government spending in the years leading up to 2007–08 – the end of the Howard era – "stands out, along with the growth in spending under the Whitlam Government in 1974–75 and the increased spending following the recessions in 1982–83 and 1990–91." The Treasury paper revealed in all its glory the trend of giving individuals money rather investing it in traditional government areas such as health and education.

In Peter Costello's last budget, 41 per cent of the spending (in a booming economy) was on social security and welfare, and just 18 per cent was on health. Howard's big health outlay was on a subsidy for private health insurance, not for the hospital system. While user-pays might have always been a central tenet of liberal belief, the integrity of this principle was severely compromised by the constant hand-outs. These also sat oddly with the fact that Costello had alerted us to the looming problem of our ageing population, which would require more spending on government services, particularly health.

The picture was similar for education. Tiffen and Gittins point out that it its

> public share of total education spending Australia was already at the low end of the spectrum in 1995 before the Howard government came to power. But it became even more so [12 points below the average] in the following ten years, making the private share of education spending third highest among [seventeen other advanced democracies including the United States, Canada, Japan and the countries of Western Europe].
>
> Much of this was to do with the growth in private schools, and that points to another of its distinctive features, the public subsidy of private providers. One-fifth of Australian public spending on education goes to private institutions, almost double the overall average of 10.5 per cent, a particularly high figure when it is remembered that private universities have a negligible presence in Australia.

Tiffin and Gittins found the data on universities even more dramatic:

> In 1995 Australia was already at the lower end of the countries in terms of the public share of tertiary education spending, 13 points below the average. After another decade, though, the public share had dropped to less than half, 48 per cent, and Australia was then 26 points below the average.
>
> This reflected an increased emphasis on private funding, but also – uniquely among these developed democracies – a reduction in real terms in public spending on tertiary education. In 2005, Australia spent 0.8 per cent of GDP compared with an average of 1.1 per cent … In the other countries for which we have data, public spending on tertiary education was up by 30 per cent in real terms over the decade 1995–2005. Only Australia's decreased.

The economy, meanwhile, continued to transform during the Howard years under pressure of the change that had started with the floating of the dollar and now increased with the new mining boom. Australians had grown accustomed to a lower Australian dollar and saw it as a good thing, but the dollar started to rise, reflecting record prices for commodities. Services and tourism, which had expanded dramatically under the low dollar, started to contract. Traditional manufacturing continued its decline. The privatisation of government instrumentalities saw large numbers of skilled workers leave the safety of government employment and go out on their own, setting their own price for their work. By 2007 Australia seemed to have become a world dominated by "subbies": independent contractors whose numbers spread from the building industry to all the other industries that were being deregulated or outsourced. John Howard was able to claim them, too, as part of his battler tribe.

The mining boom led politics further away from fiscal restraint and good policy and towards idolatry of the hip-pocket. The first decade of the new century saw political parties shovelling money out the door in unprecedented tax cuts that helped fuel a once-in-a-lifetime consumption boom. It did not suit politicians to talk anymore about "the power of the markets." Instead the quest was to make the world a more certain place, with slogans such as the Howard promise that he would govern "for all of us," which implied that the government had Australians covered. At the same time, the Coalition mouthed the rhetoric of free markets and competition, particularly when it came to the workplace. Yet economic reform was increasingly wrapped in so many blankets of compensation and political bribery as to be largely unrecognisable. Consider the GST: to get it through, everyone was compensated with tax cuts or increased benefits. First-home buyers received a special grant which was intended to offset the one-off increase in building inputs, but which is still with us today. Food was exempted, as were other day-to-day items. Politicians still talked about reform, but the extent of government intervention in the economy was slowly back on an upward path, concealed by the fact that Howard so often put the intervention in the form of a government subsidy of the private sector. Economic change became something that politicians could get kudos for if they got the bribes right, not because they had convinced voters that the change would be in the long-term national interest.

By the time of the 2007 election, interest rates had been set by the markets for over twenty-five years. It was a sign of how the political debate had regressed, or perhaps failed to come to terms with the deregulatory push in the first place, that discussion of rate movements was still framed by the question of politicians' influence over them – whether politicians could or should bully the Reserve Bank or the banks about their decisions.

At that same election, voters made it clear that the process of freeing up wage-setting had gone far enough and rejected Howard's attempts to push it further with his WorkChoices legislation.

The election would also see another longstanding issue about how we are governed come to the fore. Hawke and Keating had found themselves increasingly bumping up against the states in the reform processes they unleashed. Howard's preference for giving money to individuals or the private sector through subsidies, rather than to state-controlled institutions such as hospitals, meant he had largely avoided confrontation with the states. But by 2007 he, too, was being forced to confront the difficulties of the federation.

Health and education were the obvious areas. The community expected the federal government to fund the health system properly, yet it was controlled by the states. The long-ignored dilemma prompted an intense debate within the Coalition over health policy, which gave rise to Tony Abbott's proposal to bypass the states and put individual hospitals under local community control. There had also been shouts from business for years for government to do something about infrastructure. The ports and transport hubs in major cities had to be addressed. But while there had been some infiltration by federal governments into road and rail systems over the years, it had tended to end at the fringes of large cities, where the states – which did not have the necessary funds – took over.

Enter Kevin Rudd, who made a renovated federalism a central feature of his election campaign. So many of Rudd's political and policy instincts were right in 2007. He recognised that voters now rarely drew a distinction between the powers and responsibilities of state and federal governments: they just wanted things fixed. His pitch was to break down the divide by taking the federal government squarely into the realm of service-delivery, in areas such as health and transport. He had a proposal for doing this with hospitals, and one for doing it with infrastructure that looked "cooperative first, confrontational second." He also promised an education "revolution," which would reverse the fall in funding under the Coalition: "a substantial and sustained increase in the quantity of our investment, and the quality of our education at every level of education, from early childhood to mature age." This wasn't about a takeover of schools and universities, but rather a huge increase in federal funds: tax write-offs for parents on education expenses, massive investment in computers in schools, more subsidies and scholarships for university students.

Rudd was "Kevin from Queensland," the bureaucratic nerd who was "here to help." There was no more discussion about the withdrawal of the state. Government was not just here to give you hand-outs but, once again, to look after you properly. Rudd made public servants fashionable, even trendy. He spoke the incomprehensible language of bureaucracy, and for a time people found that engaging and endearing. Here was what we needed, someone who actually understood the system and could get it working for us. Not only that, he was taking personal responsibility for fixing it all. He wasn't going to sidestep the complex issue of funding public hospitals by simply increasing subsidies to private ones. If he couldn't get the states to fix their hospital systems, the federal government itself would pay.

Rudd's 2007 election platform offered a return to large-scale government intervention, institutional solutions to policy problems and a new take on federal–state relations. These were three places where Howard just couldn't go. But it was also a place that planted a huge bullseye on Rudd's forehead, saying: "Blame me." Only someone possessed of remarkable hubris would have taken on federal–state reform, something that had defeated, or been cunningly avoided by, three of our most politically talented prime ministers: Hawke, Keating and Howard.

Rudd failed from the start to enlist the states: to persuade them that there was a mutual interest in coming up with a new model for the health system. His political successes had always been about "people power." He won the Labor leadership, despite his caucus colleagues' dislike of him, because he was popular on morning television. He enjoyed record levels of popularity as prime minister simply because he was the nerd who seemed to be trying to get things done. It all fell to pieces, however, because he lacked the organisational skills and persuasive ability required to win over the professionals with whom he had to deal on the big reform issues. Despite coming out of the state bureaucracy and therefore claiming to know all about federal–state relations, he did not have the political savvy to propose deals on which the states were prepared to negotiate seriously.

The ambition of Rudd's agenda, and the fact that it, at least briefly, changed our expectations of the role of government, was a breath of fresh air in 2007. But he was to disappoint voters on climate change and become stuck in no-man's-land on health reform. There were questions of competence in the way services were administered that quickly saw cynicism about the public sector re-emerge. Perhaps the very ambition of his agenda made voters tougher on Rudd when he couldn't deliver it. His high standing in the polls through 2008 and 2009 slumped in 2010. Emboldened and alarmed by the reversal of his poll standing, Rudd's colleagues, sick of the autocratic way he ran the government, moved against him. Yet, as it transpired, if there was one entitlement that Australians believed they had above all others, it was to decide who would be their prime minister. The caucus move to override that right would be catastrophic for Labor.

Kevin Rudd raised voters' expectations to a risky degree. He suggested that he could make government respond to our needs. It was a change from the politics of personal entitlement of John Howard. Labor gradually introduced tighter means testing on measures such as the baby bonus and private health insurance rebates, but Rudd was reluctant to challenge head-on the idea of entitlement that Howard had embedded in Australian governance. There things sat until September 2008 and the onset of the global financial crisis.

In the scramble to respond, Australians got the full monty of government intervention: cash payments to households, support for industry through building programs, support for the financial system through guarantees. Many of these measures replicated the protections that had existed in the original Australian settlement and been dismantled in the era of deregulation. There wasn't protection for industries in the form of tariffs this time around, but there were cash payments.

Instead of the raft of legislation and controls that had once provided support and comfort to voters, the government had just one lever at its disposal: the budget. It used its financial resources and capacity to borrow, confident that the bottom line would quickly recover. After all, for the previous five years, the mining boom had repeatedly delivered billions of dollars in extra revenue. Saving Australians from the world meant going into deficit: it meant not offsetting the big fall in tax collections while also engaging in extra spending. Budget surpluses had by now become a talisman of good government for both sides of politics, seen to equal good economic management. One could almost hear a sharp intake of breath among journalists in the press gallery as the treasurer was asked in the early months of the crisis whether the times might actually call for going into (gulp) deficit.

The government's measures to stave off recession and keep confidence buoyed were supposed to be one-offs that could be quickly implemented and equally quickly unwound. The reality proved more difficult. Having put financial guarantees in place for the banking system, it was hard to take them away. Many voters – rather than being grateful for the cash hand-outs and understanding that they were designed to keep consumers in shops and, therefore, the economy ticking over – were cynical about getting money for nothing.

Perhaps most significantly, the program that sought to double up the policy goals of providing employment and improving the insulation of Australian housing exposed a harsh reality: the changes of the previous two decades had left the federal bureaucracy with no direct experience of running service-delivery programs. This lack of experience also left the federal government at the mercy of the states to administer the huge out-lay on school buildings. The vision of seamless, cooperative federalism that had been a central plank of Rudd's 2007 election victory stumbled even before he ran into trouble on hospital reform.

By the time Rudd was toppled, there was a perfect storm brewing of confused expectations about what government and politicians could do for us. For a society built on state paternalism there is no deeper expecta-tion than that the government is in control of events. In the experience of most voters, the only true governmental crisis to that point had been the last days of the Whitlam government.

In 2010, the government walked away from its policy on climate change, an issue that had been so important to voters in 2007 and which Kevin Rudd had said was the "greatest moral, economic and environmen-tal challenge of our generation." Rudd was declaring surrender because the Opposition wouldn't support him, rather than taking the question to voters in a double-dissolution election. Business, which had either been aboard the Hawke–Keating reform cart or pacified by various bouts of industrial relations reform by the Howard government, was now openly critical of the Rudd government's economic management as a result of a proposed new mining tax. The assault, particularly from the miners, was not only massive and well funded, but, for many voters, something new.

The Opposition relentlessly attacked Labor's competence to deliver services, run the economy and keep boat people out of the country.

Bipartisanship on major reforms in the 1980s had started to break down when John Howard came to office, particularly under the Labor leadership of Simon Crean. When Labor won in 2007, the Coalition scarcely acknowledged the government's mandate, despite the sweeping nature of its victory. It had learnt a brutal form of politics when it was in government and now turned it on Labor. Howard had not only created a battler tribe of voters, but also, according to the writer Norman Abjorensen, brought about a "tribalisation" of the Liberal Party itself. Abjorensen says the Liberals' dislike of Labor:

> went from the political to the visceral; not a single appointment under Howard had the slightest tinge of bipartisanship about it – a striking contrast with the Rudd–Gillard government's appointment of former Liberal politicians, including Nelson, Downer and Bruce Baird to various posts.
>
> The ... unprecedented interjection in parliament directed at the prime minister from the advisers' boxes by Abbott's chief of staff, Peta Credlin, is simply a manifestation of the new Liberal tribalism; it is anger, resentment and frustration all rolled into one, underpinned by an intense loathing, verging on hatred.

Tony Abbott won the leadership of the Coalition from Malcolm Turnbull in December 2009, when Turnbull was attempting to reach a bipartisan position with the government on an issue of significant government intervention in the economy, the emissions trading system. The shift from Turnbull's willingness to negotiate to Abbott's blanket opposition (a position he had reached only a couple of months earlier) finished off not only the proposals for a carbon trading scheme, but broke the back of the government's authority.

In June 2010, Australians woke to find they had a new prime minister they hadn't voted for, who was telling them that the government had "lost its way," but was unable to say how that had happened or whether she was going to lead them somewhere different. There were weeks of uncertainty about when Julia Gillard would go to the polls to seek "legitimacy," and weeks of uncertainty about how she would fix, as she had promised to, the government's three big policy problems: asylum seekers, the mining tax and climate change.

Governments, in our general experience, were competent and stable. We weren't like one of those European countries, or Japan or Thailand, where governments, formed by alliances of small parties or racked by corruption scandals, were always falling. In such countries, voters tended to greet the comings and goings of governments with a shrug of the shoulders. Similarly, we hadn't experienced the perpetual battle between the US Congress and the president over the budget or specific reforms that American voters take as the norm.

Julia Gillard sought to resolve the question of her legitimacy with an early election. We remember the 2010 election campaign now for the devastating leaks that reinforced images of her as duplicitous. We remember her statement a couple of days before the election that there would be "no carbon tax under the government I lead." But for the purposes of my argument about entitlement and expectations, the 2010 campaign was significant for things not so widely remembered.

Since the 1980s, big tax cuts and hand-outs had been the rock on which election campaigns were built. As the Howard government grew older and older, the size of the cuts, and the size of the election promises, became bigger and bigger. Labor had matched Howard's huge 2007 tax-cuts promises — some of which would not be delivered until years into the next parliament. But the global financial crisis, and Labor's determination to spare us from it, changed all that. Not only had the Rudd government spent everything in the war chest, but a slow recovery from the crisis, and the impact of massive investment write-offs in the resources sector, meant there was no prospect of it being refilled anytime soon.

The 2010 campaign was therefore the first in living memory when voters were asked to back a side not on the basis of what might be in it for them and their hip pocket, but on the basis of policy differences, such as they were. A sustainable population size and immigration were early hot topics. There were lingering questions about carbon pricing (and Gillard's dopey early suggestion of a "citizens' assembly") and the mining tax. The parties were for or against the National Broadband Network; for or against different education policies; for or more-or-less for an industrial relations status quo. The Coalition tried to trump Labor's paid parental-leave scheme with one of its own, but only managed to confuse people about how it would be funded. In the unique political circumstances of 2010, without a sack of promised entitlements, everyone found it hard to focus on policy, turning instead to the character of the leaders. Gillard had her problems with the Rudd coup. Abbott's attitude to women was also a problem, whether he was urging them to save their virginity for marriage, or making bad jokes suggesting that when it came from Julia Gillard, "no" didn't mean "no."

A very different election campaign produced an equally different parliamentary result: for the first time in almost seventy years, a minority government was formed. It turns out that Australians loathe minority government, and we now had one with a credibility problem and which was cornered by the parliament, the states, business and the media. In 2012 it is hard to find people who are not angry about at least one aspect of the present dispensation, be it Gillard herself, Labor in minority government, the role of the Greens, the role of the independents or the uncertain parliament. This prime minister, this parliament, these minor parties and independents were not what we expected. A government that spends every day protecting itself can hardly be looking after us.

Commentators speak often of how Gillard lost the trust of voters, but the social researcher Rebecca Huntley says there is something more powerful at work.

They see her as having delivered minority government by having knifed Rudd prematurely and running a bad election campaign. The Australian electorate doesn't like lots of different parties controlling the situation. We like a feeling of one political party with an agenda that it is able to pursue but with checks and balances.

So it's not just that we see Gillard as a backstabber who brought down an elected prime minister, it is that we see her as the very reason we have minority government. Gillard has become the embodiment of a crushing number of uncertainties and disappointed expectations, both about politics and Australia's future, which make voters uncomfortable – and in some cases angry.

The Coalition's long-time pollster Mark Textor says that voters have been hit by a "rolling series of uncertainties":

> There is a deep, structural economic uncertainty. People are worried about their savings and their job. There is a performance uncertainty. That is, an increasing uncertainty about whether governments can, let alone will, deliver …
>
> There is uncertainty about the present financial situation and the international economy, as Europe has continued to dominate the headlines.
>
> There is a new sense of political uncertainty created by the act of MPs moving to chop a first-time prime minister on the back of bad polling, and a deep structural uncertainty about the nature of politics when it is played on an "all bets are off" basis.
>
> There is structural uncertainty about policy, which started with Gillard's talk during the election campaign of a summit to develop a consensus on climate change [and] then morphed into the deal with the Greens on a carbon tax.
>
> There is additional uncertainty about the nature of the parliament and how it operates.

When Textor speaks of voters' financial uncertainty, this encompasses the "cost of living," which is cited on all sides of politics as the issue that most disgruntles voters beyond the state of politics itself. We are angry that politicians seem to be out of touch with the pressures we're under.

The cost of living used to be code for high inflation. Yet our inflation rate is historically benign. The new reference points are energy prices and housing, and these are both areas where governments have lost the control they once had. Large parts of the electricity market have been either deregulated or privatised, and whereas governments once subsidised new electricity infrastructure, now they don't (and couldn't afford to), so the cost pops up on our quarterly statements. Huntley says that even when politicians say they will try to keep a lid on prices with a mechanism such as Rudd's Grocery Watch scheme, we know that they can't really do anything, but we blame them anyway, in effect twice – both for prices going up and for their impotence to do anything about it.

Deregulation put the biggest price signals in our economy – interest rates and the exchange rate – largely out of the government's reach, and therefore out of our control. Yet we still expect politicians to "do something" about these, while absorbing any benefits from these market movements as our just entitlement. How many Australians link the huge fall in the price of cars, televisions and other goods we buy from overseas manufacturers in the past five years with the decision to float the dollar, and, as a result, the dollar now being so high? The Treasury secretary Martin Parkinson pointed out in a speech in March 2012 that the high exchange rate, while hurting the non-mining sectors, is one way the benefits of the resource boom have spread across the economy, boosting living standards through cheaper imports.

It does not help that we are always being told we are worse off than we were before. Bills go up, so people tend to believe it. Yet research conducted for the News Limited tabloid newspapers last year by the National Centre for Social and Economic Modelling showed that the average Australian household had $23 *a day* more disposable income than five years earlier as a result of higher wages, income tax cuts and increased welfare.

Mark Textor says that everyone, no matter their circumstances, is vulnerable to uncertainty:

> because even if you are doing better, say you are living in Western Australia, you are still aware that your finances are stretched, albeit more well funded now.
>
> Because your financial horizons are better, you have stretched to them and so even though you are better off than someone else, you are still feeling stretched. The uncertainty becomes, how do I maintain this lifestyle? I'm more leveraged now. Even though I have a higher income, I'm more leveraged.
>
> On the eastern seaboard, when you are comparing yourself to the rest of the world, you say, "Well, yes but I've got greater needs. I've promised my children a better education, I've promised my wife a nice holiday. I've promised myself a progression in life. I've promised myself better circumstances. I still feel that competitive pressure more than ever."
>
> So it's not sufficient if you live in WA, or you live in the east, to simply compare yourself to the rest of the world. It's not sufficient to say "We're okay," because a relativity is not a comfort.

Rebecca Huntley says that Australians are confused about the implications of opening up the country:

> In previous times consumers understood that we'd get things like fashion and books months later than the rest of the world because we were at the ends of the earth. But the fact Australia is now so intimately associated with the rest of the world means that if something goes awry elsewhere, we lose our super. We are suddenly aware of what other countries enjoy from the retail sector and service providers.

She recounts someone in a focus group noting that you could buy a global brand at half the price online as in a shop here. Instead of seeing that as good, he railed against the high domestic price. The impact of the global financial crisis on people's superannuation savings has been particularly important, Huntley says, in establishing the idea that we are "only getting the downside" of being part of the world. "People are more educated [and] outward-looking, but also more aggressive. Opening our society has fed our sense of entitlement."

Thus, when the Gillard government finally got legislation through parliament earlier this year that imposed a means test on the private health insurance rebate, the *Australian* reported the reaction of a family in Adelaide which earned a combined income of more than $258,000 and, as a result, would lose the 30 per cent health insurance subsidy they were receiving from the federal government. "It's ridiculous – the better we do, the more the government takes," the woman said. "Every time we try to get ahead and don't rely on the welfare system, we get a guarantee they'll hit us again." This battler was oblivious to the idea that the rebate might have been just another form of welfare.

The two sides of politics have now adopted very different approaches to explain the confusing times in which we live. The government's message is, in the broad, "It's complicated." The Opposition's message is, "It's simple."

"It's complicated" is a particularly vulnerable message (whether or not it be true) because it relies on people trusting the government to fix it, when voters clearly don't trust the government, and the government seems unable to explain why it can, or can't, fix it in the first place.

Tony Abbott has a much simpler set of messages: "Stop the boats." "Stop the taxes." "Stop the debt." "Stop the NBN." That he is yet to reveal any credible initiative that clearly will "stop the boats" is apparently beside the point, just as it is unclear how he will repeal both the mining tax and the carbon tax but not all the things they fund. The Coalition's website tells us that Labor is responsible for a raft of cost-of-living increases, including a rise in the price of fruit and vegetables.

Huntley says: "We get a little bit [showing up in our research] about people saying, 'Well, he [Abbott] kind of thinks we're idiots.' 'He kind of says he'll solve this problem by stopping the boats and solve this problem by getting rid of the carbon tax.' People know it can't be that simple, so there is a sense in which people will see through these platitudes that of course as an Opposition leader it's much easier to present to the public than it is in government."

Tony Abbott is the prime minister in waiting. He and his party have attacked the interventions made on behalf of the country during the global financial crisis, and he has framed his messages about what he will do in terms of how he will stop the intrusion of government (and boat people) into people's lives. The ongoing crisis of the Gillard government has meant there have been few periods in which Abbott has been pressured to spell out a coherent alternative. So we don't really know what our choice of expectations is in the immediate future.

In recent months, Abbott has begun to make some "headland" speeches outlining some of his views on government and policy. In doing so, he replicates the approach of his political hero, John Howard, in 1995. He not only replicates the strategy, he also replicates much of the message. For Abbott's speeches call on his audience to hark back to the "golden" days of the Howard government and promise both more entitlements – a more expensive child-care system and the measures funded by the mining tax (without the mining tax) – and less government spending.

By far the more interesting – and realistic – contribution to the debate from within the Coalition has been from Abbott's shadow treasurer, Joe Hockey, who gave a speech in London in April about entitlement. His message was simple: the Age of Entitlement is over. Much of the speech dealt with the problems of the debt-laden European and US economies, but there was also a clear message about where Hockey thinks Australia should go. He argued that Western democracies have been reluctant to wind back universal access to payments and entitlements despite ageing populations and the prospect that our children will not enjoy the living standards we do. Politicians of all persuasions have been promising more and more, despite not having the revenue to pay for it and, as a result, many countries have built up huge levels of government debt.

"The social contract between government and its citizens needs to be urgently and significantly redefined," Hockey said.

> The reality is that we cannot have greater government services and more government involvement in our lives coupled with significantly lower taxation. As a community we need to redefine the responsibility of government and its citizens to provide for themselves, both during their working lives and into retirement ... [There needs to be] clear thinking about which services should be provided by governments and whether government-funded services should be entirely free or have some affordable co-payment.

Hockey's argument is that government spending has to be determined by government revenue. Furthermore, in deciding the new social contract, Western countries, including Australia, must take into account that they are competing economically with Asian countries, which have much lower levels of spending on their citizens.

His position raises interesting questions about the next Coalition government, beyond the obvious ones about the conflicting messages from its spokesmen. Tony Abbott has spent the last eighteen months appealing to Howard's battlers. At the core of that appeal is the idea of entitlement. If Hockey is right, it won't just be a question of cutting back entitlements, but of a government telling Australians that we have to reconceive what we expect of government itself.

*

It is wrong to see the anger of the last few years as a "one-off," which might go away at the next election. The things we are angry about betray the changes that have been taking place over recent decades. As we have seen, politicians no longer control interest rates, the exchange rate, or wages, prices or industries that were once protected or even owned by government. Voters are confused about what politicians can do for them in such a world. While the levers available to government to protect us have been removed, the expectation that we will still be protected has been fed by the failure of our politicians to explain their new impotence. Our political expectations are still driven by the settlement made at federation.

The failure of our political discourse over the past two decades to recognise the implications of dismantling the Australian settlement for our long-held ideas of government leaves us ill-equipped in 2012 to deal with the big questions of governance. These questions concern our relationship with the world; a changed budgetary situation; problems in the federation; and the level of government intervention in our society and economy.

Globalisation has made us more exposed to changes taking place around the world. We are confronted by the spectre of Europe and the US spending at least next the decade experiencing conflict and constraint, if not actual decline. At the same time, Asia, with its very different take on the role of the state, is on the rise. Western countries are now being forced to confront what their governments, under massive budgetary pressures, can afford to provide.

At home, both sides of politics are committed to spending and taxing trajectories that are not feasible even in the medium term. It's not just that politicians won't be able to afford to offer more tax cuts in the future; they will either have to increase taxes or cut their spending commitments, including ones they have already made.

In March, Martin Parkinson outlined the new reality of Australia's finances. Since the global financial crisis, he said, tax revenue as a proportion of the economy had fallen by four percentage points and it "is not expected to recover to its pre-crisis level for many years." His comments point to a disconnection in the established relationship between the rate of growth in the economy and the rate of growth in tax collections.

Strong economic growth no longer necessarily means strong growth in tax revenue. With the ending of the asset boom of the 2000s, capital gains tax collections have been hit hard. Households are also more cautious in their spending, which hits indirect taxes such as the GST (with implications for state budgets). While the resources sector accounts for about a fifth of our corporate profits, it only generates about one-tenth of company tax receipts because high levels of investment attract big tax deductions. Finally, the historically high Australian dollar is lowering profits in other parts of the economy, and therefore reducing how much tax those sectors pay.

Implicit in Parkinson's message, as the *Sydney Morning Herald*'s economics editor Ross Gittins points out, is that:

> all these things are just elements of a more fundamental explanation for the budget's new growth/tax disconnect: the Howard government's decision to cut the rates of income tax for eight years in a row.
>
> This has robbed the income-tax scale of its propensity to bracket creep. It also represented a significant shift in the federal tax mix, greatly reducing reliance on personal income tax and greatly increasing reliance on capital gains tax and, particularly, company tax. Get the point? This switch was made at a time when, for all the reasons we've discussed, the level of non-income tax revenue was artificially high. Now those temporary factors have evaporated, leaving us with a badly wounded tax base.

Gittins points out that both sides of politics are ultimately responsible for this problem, as Labor matched the Coalition's tax cuts. Now both sides of politics must reap what they have sown.

The changing tax base is also a problem for the states. Their budget positions are already in a much worse state than the federal government's and they ultimately deliver so many of the services that we expect of government. We have come full circle: from the time when the states established what they thought would be a small federal government to the states now being reliant on the federal government to prop them up financially if they wish to keep delivering the services they so desperately seek to control.

Our politicians will at last have to sort out just who does what, and how best to let that happen. Our leaders know it, too. Tony Abbott went to the trouble of including in his book *Battlelines* some draft legislation for a referendum that would give the federal government power to override state legislation. "It wouldn't abolish the states," Abbott said, "but, because Commonwealth law prevails over state law to the extent of any inconsistency, it would mean that they could not jeopardise policy in areas where the national government was determined to intervene." This from a leader of a party that has always advocated states' rights.

Australians will be forced in the next decade to consider what level of government intervention we really want, and what form it should take. That will require us to forge a much more explicit new settlement, a much clearer social contract than the one we have had to date. We must assess what level of government intervention works in an open economy and how best to deliver it. We will have to go back to the idea that government assistance is on a needs – not an entitlements – basis and work out which needs we are prepared to support. Our politicians will have to face up to the question of what governments can realistically promise – and what they can no longer pledge to provide – and change their messages accordingly.

Mark Textor says, "Australians have trodden water before, but they have never been so far out to sea and without someone they trust pointing to a horizon, saying, 'That is where we have to swim.' People talk about the 'vision thing.' To me it's not a vision, it's the horizon that people seek."

He put me in mind of the journey of the sixteenth-century explorer Ferdinand Magellan. Fourteen months after leaving Seville, crossing the Atlantic and tracking down the east coast of South America, and losing two of his ships along the way to mutiny and shipwreck, Magellan sailed through the strait at the bottom of South America and entered the Pacific Ocean on 28 November 1520. His next landfall was in the Marianas Islands, east of the Philippines, three months and 12,600 miles later. Go and look at a globe to see how far that is, and how much blue water lies in every direction. I often wonder how he kept order on his too-little ships, imbuing his crew with the belief that they would find land in a safe and hospitable place, in a world that on maps was drawn as having an edge and was believed to be inhabited by dragons and other strange creatures.

A little like Magellan, we've reached the end of the known world in our political discussion of the past couple of decades. Australia's voyage is nowhere near as scary as Magellan's, but we lack a captain with the skills to persuade us that they know the way. We are fighting so much among ourselves about the personal qualities of our leaders that we cannot rationally discuss the options open to us. And we don't really know where we are headed or, indeed, where we want to go.

ACKNOWLEDGMENTS

Dedicated to my beloved angry Australian, Alan Ramsey.

My thanks to Margaret Swieringa for taking it upon herself to volunteer some excellent and helpful research.

Correspondence

Sophie Cunningham

Back in the 1970s, when I was doing Year 12 biology, we studied a famous experiment. Apparently, baby rhesus monkeys deprived of a mother would choose a fur "mother" that they could cuddle over a metal "mother" which had milk to feed them, even if they starved to death. When spikes were hidden in the fur, inflicting various forms of distress on the babies, they would still attempt to cling to the fur mother. It was only a few years ago that I began to wonder: why was this experiment considered necessary, given that what was proven was what most of us would assume? And who came up with the idea of putting the spikes in the fur?

In China Miéville's novel *The City and the City*, two distinct cultures and cities survive, in the same geographical location, by "unseeing" the other. "Seeing" is a form of heresy. Anna Krien's *Us and Them* is an exercise in a similar heresy as she opens her (and our) eyes to look directly at the lives of the animals that live with us and around us, that are bred by us and killed by us. She's not the first writer and thinker to do this, and she won't be the last. But each time an essay such as this is written, it becomes harder for all of us to "unsee" the plight of animals.

There are many confronting moments in the essay, too many to list here, but Krien doesn't just rely on images of violence to make her point. She also refers to the biologist Edward O. Wilson's description of the period that will follow the massive extinction of species that is currently taking place as "The Age of Loneliness," which is the kind of phrase that chimes out, and then leaves a hollow silence. Reading *Us and Them* is an emotional business. Indeed, Krien encourages emotional responses with an approach to her subject that is personal, not abstract. As a writer she's made the right decision in doing this: the reason that our killing and sometimes torturing of animals on a mass scale has been normalised is because of our refusal to connect to the subject on an emotional level. Abstraction is, if you like, another form of "unseeing," or, perhaps, "unfeeling."

The other night, at the end of a long, sad day during which I read Krien's essay, I was listening to the radio news as a particularly grisly war crime was being reported on. *How do people let this happen?* I thought. *Why are they unable to speak up?* I was thinking about collusion and the way it allows so much horror, violent and otherwise, to be visited upon human beings. And then a flash of the footage of cattle being slaughtered in Indonesian abattoirs came into my head. It was this same footage – shown on *Four Corners* almost a year ago – that led Krien to visit Indonesia and consider the plight of the cattle and the workers, and the machinations of the beef industry. Then an older memory returned, one that's haunted me on and off for some twenty years. I was in Sapa, in Vietnam, in the early '90s, and I saw a group of men kick a pig to death in the village square. It happened because the pig had struggled and escaped when it was being forced into a cage on the back of a motorcycle. As it was kicked and punched, it screamed in terror and in pain (sounds that were uncannily human, I must say) while I, and other tourists, stood and watched, uncertain as to what to do.

In general I've been finding that the boundaries I'd put up between different parts of my life have started falling away as I've grown older. I can't eat a plate of slow-cooked lamb without wondering about the treatment of the lamb when it was alive. I can't avoid thinking about the fact that the attentive, loving and curious intelligence of my cats is not a quality I have given them – it's a quality that they brought to our relationship and that they share with most animals. They are, to be blunt, my intimate friends, so what does it mean when I eat creatures similar to them? Creatures similar to me?

After decades of holding these thoughts at bay, they've lodged themselves in my brain and there's no shaking them. It's an awakening of sorts, and while it's been in train for a long time and influenced several writing projects, it was *Us and Them* which meant I couldn't, for a moment longer, escape the following admission: I collude, all meat eaters collude, in an industry based on the suffering and terror of fellow beings. The fact that these beings aren't human doesn't change that, and nor does the spurious notion that a human being's life is worth more than an animal's. I'm ashamed it's taken me so long to allow myself to accept this.

Krien seems to know such realisations take a long time, and the essay ends on a poignant note of fragility, age and understanding. The implication is that as you get older, you start to understand that your body may fail you at any moment. As a consequence you see animals as kin and there is the realisation that there is no us and them. There is only us.

Sophie Cunningham

US AND
THEM

Geoff Russell

Anna Krien's brilliant essay, Us and Them, plumbs the depths of three kinds of contact between us and other animals, which she calls killing, testing and hunting. All involve one-on-one violence and are a stark contrast to the empathy which many feel with the companion or other animals they meet. But as I read the essay, a couple of questions relentlessly hunted, tested and sometimes killed my attention. The first is about eyes. Do killer-tester-hunters look their victims in the eye? Krien gives eyes many a mention. They are gouged and poked, they dart and observe. But they are looked *at* rather than *into*.

Perhaps it's the very intensity of the interaction that makes eye contact considered rude in some cultures, but in the West it's what we do. Film plots frequently turn on eye contact. The clichéd lovers across a crowded room, the villain realising he's been glimpsed in the act, or the riveting eyeline through a rifle scope in the unforgettable jungle confrontation between good and evil in *Platoon*. Physical contact beyond a handshake is generally reserved for a small inner circle of friends and family, but eye contact involves us in interpersonal relations with vastly more people. Can we trust a person who won't look us in the eye? Perhaps that depends on whether we ourselves can lie with a straight gaze and steady voice. Is eye contact more revealing of intent than praise, a caress or a gift? I suspect so.

And with animals? What about eye contact between us and them? Krien has missed it. Eye contact doesn't happen with all species, but when it happens, it can transfix. In any event, it's all you will get from a wild duck. I had a lesson about ducks and eye contact in my first days of rescuing the wounded victims of duck shooters over twenty years ago. A friend with years of Fauna Rescue experience told me that avoiding eye contact was the key to getting close enough to have a chance at rescuing the injured birds. Ducks with shotgun injuries sufficient to stop them flying will hide where they can. In swamp vegetation they can easily become invisible and they know it. You can walk within a metre and be oblivious to their presence. But make eye contact and they will be off. Diving and swimming and popping up in another clump of vegetation in some random direction. Broken legs won't stop them. Broken wings won't stop them. They are fleeing as if their life depends on it, because it normally does.

Perhaps our capacity to recognise eye contact so well stems from the same place as a duck's. For millions of years before we added prostheses to our limbs and learned to kill with intent, we were cat food. The predator that fails to recognise having been seen will miss a meal, but the stakes are higher for prey.

I was sceptical that a bird with a brain the size of a walnut could decipher eye contact with a person, but a duck does. The trick is to scan with a panning motion and try to keep any duck you glimpse on the edge of your vision. Then walk towards a point a metre or so to one side. Pounce when close. Don't be diffident.

A thousand years ago another Anna Krien, or more likely a male counterpart, could have written a similar essay to Us and Them, but about slaves. They were hunted like ducks, for pleasure if not for food, and they were sold like cattle. The same was still true 160 years ago, but the tide was turning. Gentlemen slave traders with silken manners and a horde of bastard children felt the need to try to justify their activities. We still have slave traders and flesh traffickers, but these days they make no pretence of civility. The evil is naked. Bald of face and steady of gaze, it looks its victims in the eye without flinching. Probably because evil looks at eyes and not into them. Perhaps in another 200 years, people will still be killing and hunting animals but there too the pretence will have vanished. Gratuitous killing will be seen for what it is.

But there are also relationships with animals well beyond the intimate. They were the second shadow that plagued my reading of Krien's essay. They are beyond eye contact and beyond the nuzzle, pat and stroke. These are missing from Krien's very personal essay. Just as there is a split-second when both parties realise eye contact has been made, there is a similarly brief but one-sided instant when our reasoning crystallises an idea. When the complex becomes blindingly obvious. In the quantitative sciences, it is called an *Aha!* or *Eureka* moment. Some borrow the word *epiphany* from the religious lexicon.

"Cold hard facts" is a loathsome expression for stuff which matters. What kind of person is moved by eye contact with a single distressed calf but unmoved by the knowledge that a million are taken annually from their mothers at birth and trucked long distances to slaughterhouses?

A study in the mid-1960s estimated that the weight of livestock on the planet was nineteen times that of wildlife. A more recent study estimated that it takes about ten tonnes of herbivore to support a ninety-kilogram carnivore. What has happened since the 1960s? Wildlife habitat has shrunk still further, while the realm of livestock has expanded. We are now in an era where the relationship of "us" to "them" isn't revealed by eye contact but ratios.

Put the jigsaw together and you may or may not say "Aha!", but you should at least understand why your choice to eat animals comes at the expense of not just the animals eaten but the entire web of wildlife that used to populate the planet.

The bulldozers that dragged the first spiked balls through primary Queensland rainforest on the Tully River in the 1960s killed and displaced wildlife en masse. There may have been an *Aha!* moment for the person who first realised that if you insert a huge spiked metal ball into a heavy chain using swivel hinges and drag it through the forest, the spikes will dig into the trunks of trees, the ball will climb and the resulting leverage will allow even huge trees to be felled with relative ease. The first Australians used fire; the first white Australians used ring-barking and later dynamite. But bulldozers and spiked balls made deforestation faster and cheaper. "Faster"and "cheaper": these are the drivers of history. We might wish "eye contact" was a driver, but it is so easily avoided.

The beginnings of the modern environmental movement in Australia are sometimes traced back to the Builders Labourers Federation's green bans around four hectares at Kelly's Bush in 1971. This was in the heart of Sydney's northern suburbs. Many people could eyeball those four hectares in a way that wasn't possible with the 20,000 hectares cleared to grow cattle on the Tully River. They could eyeball the bush, perhaps even make eye contact with a bird or two from twenty metres with a pair of binoculars. Did the Kelly's Bush campaigners hold barbeque fundraisers with cheap beef snags from Queensland? More than likely.

Be it biodiversity or climate change, we are constantly hampered by an inability to be moved by cold hard facts. Just like a duck, we need eye contact with impending disaster before action. Until that arrives, we sit quietly and hope our cloak of invisibility is sound of seam.

Krien's essay is beautiful but dominated by the middle of the relationship between us and them. It focuses on the space between intimacy and cold hard facts. Intimacy dominates in the halls of welfare groups and pet owners, but cold hard facts have to assert themselves to give us a chance of reducing our damaging dominance over the planet.

Geoff Russell

Thomas Ryan

In his novel *Enemies: A Love Story*, Isaac Bashevis Singer paints a bleak and damning portrait of the nature of human relationships with animals:

> As often as Herman had witnessed the slaughter of animals and fish, he always had the same thought: in their behaviour towards creatures, all men were Nazis. The smugness with which men could do with other species as he pleased exemplified the most extreme racist theories, the principle that might is right.

Much in Anna Krien's thoughtful, meditative essay serves to corroborate Singer's thesis, confirming our species' tendency to view most animals as mere things, here to serve our ends and to do with as we wish. In the early 1970s the psychologist Richard D. Ryder coined the term *speciesism* to capture this ubiquitous mindset.

Krien disabuses us of any illusions that our current treatment of animals can be construed as just – she writes that the "age-old debate is a farce – deep down we all know it." I agree with her first claim, but wish I could her share her certainty that it is something we all agree upon. Indeed, it is not borne out by our attitudes and behaviour towards animals, notwithstanding a growing apprehension that we can no longer continue with business as usual. But even here our attention and memory are not what they should be – witness the initial outrage about the footage of horrendous conditions in Indonesian abattoirs, which led to a temporary ban on the live cattle trade before the issue dropped off the radar. Subsequent revelations about abuse in a Victorian abattoir caused barely a ripple. It was as though moral fatigue had supplanted outrage – further evidence, if any was needed, that our attitudes to animals, and their importance, are highly selective and inconsistent.

This is not to mention the plainly contradictory standards applied to different animals – those animal companions who share our lives may legally be seen as property, but nevertheless are afforded greater protection than animals used for food or experimentation. And in contradiction to their legal status, those animals with whom we share our lives are invariably considered as distinct individuals and members of our households. This is why we find it incomprehensible that dogs and cats are slaughtered for food in parts of Asia, and they in turn are perplexed given that we slaughter and consume with perfect equanimity so many other creatures. Little has changed since Ruth Harrison made her telling observation in her 1964 book *Animal Machines*:

> if one person is unkind to an animal it is considered to be cruelty, but where a lot of people are unkind to animals, especially in the name of commerce, the cruelty is condoned and, once large sums of money are at stake, will be defended to the last by otherwise intelligent people.

The diminishment of concern about the live cattle trade highlighted the limitations of purely welfare-based approaches to such issues, important as these are to redress gratuitous cruelty and neglect. No one in their right mind, or with a heart, would disagree that stunning before slaughter is a vast improvement on what was occurring, but this merely raises what is a very low bar. If, as its advocates affirm, stunning renders the animals insentient, suffering, or its absence, is thereby the *sine qua non* of our ethical and moral duties towards animals. However, this pointedly fails to acknowledge that death, especially slaughter, represents a genuine harm to the individual animals. And we are left with the ironic spectacle of animal welfare organisations and their campaigners, who were rightly motivated to redress the treatment of cattle, advocating humane methods of slaughter that result in those same creatures being transformed into the ultimate "thing": meat. This sends the mixed message that unnecessary cruelty is an evil, but that animals can be treated as things for human wants.

Granted that Krien is right in believing that in our heart of hearts we acknowledge that our relations with animals are fundamentally unethical, it leaves unanswered one of the more interesting questions: how did we come to conceive of them as mere things?

In the Christian tradition, Aquinas' interpretation of the Biblical concept of dominion as sanctioning absolute human design, and Augustine's argument that animals' lack of rationality relieves us from concerning ourselves with their suffering, have been key influences. That said, there has been an alternative, albeit minority, strand that advocates stewardship and emphasises our common origin as creatures of God.

Descartes' decree that we needn't concern ourselves with the supposed suffering of animals because they are essentially non-sentient machines, although a godsend for vivisectors, is nowadays seen for the nonsense that it always was. Not so easy to discard is Kant's highly influential distinction between people and things, to whom we have direct and indirect duties respectively. For Kant, animals fall into the latter category, and this remains part of the Western world's intellectual and moral framework. It is prudent to extend kindness to animals, not for their own sake, but for what it says about our character, and because failure to do so predisposes us to treat our fellow humans badly. They are mere practice for the real game.

All these influences have been compounded by a number of further errors. First, that the interests of humans and animals are almost invariably held to be in conflict, never more so than when the topic of experimentation is discussed – Krien deftly dissects and scuttles the perennial furphy that medically we must somehow choose between our child and that animal.

Secondly, that concern for animals in a world full of human suffering is a case of misplaced priorities: that, in Krien's words, "to be pro-animal is to be anti-human." Such accusations result in the strangest bedfellows. When some years ago I had a letter opposing the live sheep trade, after the death of many thousands in transit, published in a national weekend newspaper magazine, a columnist well known for his espousal of many progressive causes took me and my fellow animal campaigners to task for getting all het up about sheep but "not giving a stuff" about refugees incarcerated in detention centres. It was as though the causes were mutually exclusive. The philosopher Mary Midgley makes the point that this peculiar attitude is the consequence of conceiving compassion as though it were a scarce resource to be judiciously rationed, rather than a force for the good that expands with use. Such criticisms also ignore the fact that those at the forefront of campaigns in the nineteenth century to improve the lot of animals were simultaneously engaged in movements seeking to protect children, oppose slavery and ameliorate the worst aspects of industrialisation.

Thirdly, that any comparison of humans and animals is inherently demeaning to the former. This is understandable when animals are often depicted as the embodiment of the worst human vices, with none of our redeeming virtues. Animal behaviourists and ethologists have somewhat corrected our prejudices on this count, in much the same way that anthropologists alerted us that distant lands were not full of primitive, bloodthirsty savages.

Our desire to identify attributes that definitively distinguish us from animals is an age-old one, but all the more remarkable in an increasingly secular world that accepts the plausibility of evolutionary explanations of our origins. Midgley observes that in fulfilling this desire we ask ourselves the wrong question – it is not what distinguishes us *from* animals but *among* animals that is the issue. At one level we accept that we are but one species among many, but at another we hanker after human uniqueness – us and them. But, as Midgley reminds us in her book *Beast and Man*, "We are not rather like animals, we *are* animals." The differences that exist are, as Darwin was always at pains to point out, differences of degree, not kind. The refusal to accept that we are fellow creatures is, I suspect, behind most of our rapaciousness, hatred and indifference towards other animals.

Acceptance would not be without significant costs to us – we would leave off slaughtering and consuming them; we would cease considering animals to be experimental objects or organ providers, accepting that the only justification for medicating or performing surgery on them would be if it was in their best interests; we would eschew all products that were animal-tested or had animal ingredients; we would attend to the wellbeing of our animal companions as vigilantly as we do to that of our children; we would seek to protect habitats and ecosystems upon which the lives of all animals depend.

Sound crazy? Such calls for radical readjustment of our ethical and moral frameworks always do, but as John Stuart Mill observed, all major shifts in these sensibilities invariably involve three stages: ridicule, discussion, adoption. We should all be grateful for Anna Krien's perspicacious contribution to the discussion.

Thomas Ryan

B.J. Coman

Anna Krien presents her material in interesting ways and holds our attention. For the greater part of her essay, she also manages a balance in judgment, something very rare in these times. Note, for instance, the subtitle of her essay, "On the Importance of Animals," not "The Rights of Animals" or some similarly loaded title, which immediately implies that the author has a particular position that they wish to promote or defend.

In fact, Krien does have an axe to grind of sorts, but it is a not so much a *position* as it is a plea for honesty when it comes to considering our treatment of animals. And I like that very much. Is there any reader of these lines who has not felt a slight uneasiness upon passing an abattoir or a tightly packed semitrailer-load of sheep heading down to the city for slaughter? This is no modern thing. Homer felt it, and so did Hesiod. In the Cyclops story, where living men are torn apart and eaten by Polyphemus, we are made to feel exactly what it might be like for animals to suffer a similar fate at the hands of humans. And, according to Hesiod, Justice begins when members of one species refrain from devouring those of another.

This question of whether our treatment of animals is *just* is the central one that Krien wishes to examine but, to me at any rate, the essay spends far too much time on the graphic depictions of animal cruelty and too little on the underlying dilemma of our being capable of pity and yet incapable of rising above the biological requirements of our animal natures and the practical requirements of our social organisation. In an age when *My Kitchen Rules*, we also devour the flesh of animals for much more than the necessities of sustenance. Our forebears were less hedonistic and, dare I say it, more *thankful* for their food. In particular, Krien might have spent more time on the *issues* underlying our treatment of animals in modern human medicine. The dilemma here is not just that one raised by Hilaire Belloc:

He prayeth best who lovest best
All creatures great and small
The streptococcus is the test
I love him most of all

but another and more thorny one: what price are we prepared to pay for a long and healthy life and where does this change into the desire for immortality?

By far the weakest part of the essay, though, is Krien's account of hunting. Here, her earlier attention to balance seems to fade. Moreover, her research has obviously been less thorough. In the first instance, she fails to note the difference between hunting pests and controlling pests. Hunting is a recreational activity that merely harvests pest populations; it does not control them. The reason is simple: as the pest population declines, the effort needed to procure a satisfactory return increases. For most of our serious mammalian pests, when the animals get scarce, fewer people bother to hunt them. Other means of control are needed and, here again, issues of animal suffering are involved. In fact, they are far more important than those involved in hunting. Compared to myxomatosis, calicivirus and 1080 poison, a minuscule proportion of the rabbit population falls to hunters in Australia.

Krien's choice of the dingo as her centrepiece species here is also unfortunate. Her reliance on conversations with a small group of dingo enthusiasts (including a few scientists) has led to a rather one-sided account. The "pure dingo" is not a biological entity, but an abstract idea.[1] Or rather, it is a wish presented as a reasoned conclusion. There is a wild canine in Australia we call the dingo. Very probably, it came from Asia, some 3500–5000 years BP. Herein lurks the first problem. How long must an animal reside in a certain area before it is considered "native"? Is 3500 years long enough? Should we regard it as being native to Australia, or native to Asia? In a thousand years, will our distant progeny regard the fox as a native animal, or the cat, or the cane toad? The general view seems to be that any organism that existed in Australia before 1788 is an indigenous species. But why should that date provide a definitive delineator of status? The tamarind tree was here long before Cook, but no one regards it as a native. Remember, too, that each individual species is not a fixed entity but a dynamic one, changing over time. This, after all, is what drives evolution. The "pure dingo" of 3000 years ago may well have been quite different from today's hypothesised "pure dingo." So all this talk of "DNA testing" is poppycock.

It is similarly unfortunate that Krien should advance the cause of the dingo (and the Tasmanian devil) as a solution to the fox and feral cat problem (is there a *proven* feral cat problem in southern Australia?). "Oh my god," she says in an exclamation of surprise, "this is a total GAME CHANGER" (her emphasis). Well, no, it's not, and that exclamation of surprise is about as convincing in her essay as when you hear it in almost every sentence uttered by teenage schoolgirls. Dingo enthusiasts (including some scientists) are now calling for the reintroduction of "pure dingoes" into national parks and wilderness areas. In my state of Victoria, farmers near the Grampians, the Otways or the Little Desert can look forward to seeing partly disembowelled sheep struggling pathetically at the tail of the mob, with flyblown wounds and all those other distressing sights associated with dog attacks. The logic for this reintroduction push is that dingoes are a natural part of the ecosystem and help to control introduced vermin animals such as cats and foxes, which prey on small native animals. Unlike "feral dogs," they will presumably lay off the sheep, chooks and endangered native mammals because they are more noble. I challenge any scientist to show me hard evidence that dingoes kill, out-compete or drive out sufficient numbers of foxes and cats to give *effective* control of harmful wildlife predation without doing serious damage to native wildlife populations. Like foxes and feral cats, dingoes eat native animals – and sheep, when they can get them. Wherever dingoes occur in Victoria, foxes and feral cats also occur, and have done so since biological records have been collected in these areas.

And then there is Krien's enthusiastic approval of Maremmas as guardians of livestock. Maremmas and other dog breeds, llamas and alpacas have been promoted as guard animals for many years in Australia, but the take-up rate of this technique by landholders has been poor. This suggests problems, since cockies are usually not slow when it comes to saving a dollar. In a 2003 report, David Jenkins from NSW Agriculture indicated that the technique had promise, but that much more data was needed via controlled experiments. At best, the guard dog idea is an additional tool in combating livestock predation, but it is by no means a complete answer to the problem.

But all this stuff on hunting "vermin" and reintroducing "native" predators is really a distraction from Krien's original purpose – to reflect upon the general *importance* of animals. In the case of hunting, it would have been far more profitable to steer clear of the "emoticon" species, dingoes, and deal with general ideas. Ortega y Gasset's famous *Meditations on Hunting* is an obvious place to begin. Then there is Aldo Leopold, one of the founders of the wildlife conservation movement in America, whose *Sand County Almanac* contains much wise reflection on hunting and the human–animal relationship in general.

The last section of the essay, on animals as beings, is another case of missed opportunities. Krien could have elaborated much more upon the distinction between a being and a "thing," but she rides off in several directions at once and the idea gets lost. For my money, this is the most important aspect of the whole human–animal problem. An appreciation of being – I mean the ontological notion – is the starting point for all subsequent ethical examinations, since it confers intrinsic worth. It is also one of the earliest philosophical ideas in the history of Western thought. Parmenides grasped it five centuries before Christ and it remained at the heart of Western philosophy for the next 2000 years. The elaboration of this ancient idea into the "Great Chain of Being" was destroyed after Descartes, Bacon, Hume and Kant. Its disappearance might well be linked to the modern view of animals merely as commodities for food or pleasure. When the notion of being is discarded, so is the question of intrinsic worth. Here, indeed, is meat for thought.

B.J. Coman

1 The interested reader is directed to B.J. Coman and E.H. Jones, "The Loaded Dog," *Quadrant*, Vol. 51, No. 11, November 2007, pp. 10–14. A more technical analysis, with original data, is available in E. Jones, "Hybridisation Between the Dingo, *Canis Lupus Dingo*, and the Domestic Dog, *Canis Lupus Familiaris*, in Victoria: A Critical Review," *Australian Mammalogy*, Vol. 31, No. 1, 2009, pp. 1–7.

Mike Letnic

Throughout the third part of Anna Krien's essay there is a deep sense of confusion over the terminology for dingoes and wild dogs and their respective identities. This confusion is crystallised in a conversation related between the author and the wild-dog biosecurity manager for the Department of Primary Industries in Victoria, concerning the identity of animals destroyed for the state's "wild dog and fox bounty" scheme. Krien concludes that "Foxes, hunting dogs gone wild, dumped dogs, dingo hybrids and dingoes are one and the same," and she accordingly uses the terms dingo and wild dog interchangeably throughout her essay. This conflation of terms clouds scientific understanding and contemporary management of the dingo and is a product of both history and the euphemistic language of bureaucracy.

"Dingo" is a word for dog derived from the language of the Aboriginal people of Sydney and was chronicled in the journal of Watkin Tench and other early writers. The term "warrigal" was also used by Sydney Aborigines to describe large wild dogs. These terms were subsequently incorporated into the pidgin language of the early NSW settlement and, along with the term "native dog," were widely used in colonial Australia. The *Gazetteer of Australia*, a compilation of official geographical place names, lists eighty-six places in New South Wales incorporating the word "dingo," sixty-three place names including the phrase "native dog," and twenty-three incorporating the name "warrigal." Evidently, the term "wild dog" did not have great historical use in New South Wales, as there are just six places in that state which feature the phrase.

Analysis of place names elsewhere in Australia suggests that "wild dog" may have its origins in Victoria and South Australia, where the majority of dog-related place names include this phrase, and "dingo" ranks second. "Dingo" is the predominant term for place names in the Northern Territory, Queensland and Western Australia. Interestingly, there is a single place named for "dingo" and four for "wild dog" recorded in the gazette for Tasmania, where dingoes have never occurred, but feral dogs have. These quite different trends in the geography of place names referring to Australia's largest land predator suggest that some of the confusion regarding terminology has historic roots in the dialects of the early colonies. However, at least three other factors also confuse the identity of this iconic Australian animal.

All species of animal that are recognised scientifically must have a formal description, usually published in a scientific journal. In general, a physical specimen known as the "type" specimen also exists somewhere in a museum. In the case of the dingo, the species description amounts merely to a paragraph in Governor Arthur Phillip's journal recounting the time he spent in New South Wales. The "description" states simply that the dingo is a vicious native dog found in New South Wales, and that when one was taken alive to England, it escaped and killed a deer. There is no type specimen anywhere in the world. From a scientific perspective this description of the dingo is deeply troubling, because there is no definitive benchmark that scientists can use to determine if an animal is or is not a dingo. Even DNA cannot resolve the issue, because of the absence of a recognised true or standard dingo genotype.

In the last ten to fifteen years there has been a push to remove the word "dingo" from public language in Australia. From what I can tell there are two reasons for this policy shift. The first stems from research performed in the 1970s and 1980s by scientists from CSIRO, which suggested a high degree of hybridisation between dingoes and feral dogs in southeastern New South Wales and Victoria, but not through the majority of the continent, where genetically pure dingoes are believed to predominate. Owing to the confusion over the genetic identity of dingoes and their hybrids in southeastern Australia, the phrase "wild dog" has been adopted as a useful cover-all term to refer to dingoes and their kin collectively.

The last reason is to my mind the most troubling. It is bureaucratic and stems from the motivation to eradicate dingoes and their wild kin. As described by Krien in her essay, dingoes, wild dogs, or whatever you want to call them, kill livestock, especially sheep. Australians have devoted a good deal of effort to exterminating these predators, including by constructing the world's longest fence and undertaking vast aerial poisoning programs. Labelling the object of this hostility with inherently Australian terms derived from indigenous languages would be troubling. It is much easier from a public relations perspective to dole out plane-loads of poison to kill wild dogs than it is to kill dingoes, warrigals or native dogs. Pointedly, the Victorian bounty program that Krien discusses was aimed at wild dogs and foxes, not dingoes. By strictly adhering to this language there are no victims of "friendly fire."

This careful use of language by the public service was brought to my attention during a brief stint I spent in the employ of the NSW Parks and Wildlife Service in the 2000s. Having grown up in New South Wales seeing dingoes and warrigals in the bush and a seemingly endless stream of documentaries by Malcolm Douglas and the Leyland Brothers, I naively wrote this term into a draft government policy document. It was also around this time that scientists were highlighting the threats posed to dingoes in New South Wales and Victoria and the important, keystone role that dingoes fulfil in Australian ecosystems by suppressing numbers of foxes. I was quickly alerted to my policy transgression and referred for a remedial meeting with a senior manager. I asked my superior why I could not use the word "dingo," although in the post-Azaria world just about everyone knew what a dingo looked like, and it was quite clear that most of the animals that the service was killing were yellow or black-and-tan dogs that looked like dingoes. He replied, "Because that is the government's policy." End of meeting.

One of the greatest challenges ahead for biodiversity conservation in Australia is to find places where wild dogs can be dingoes. After 200 years of persecution, they are endangered across large areas of the continent and will be threatened elsewhere by ever-expanding and more efficient poison-baiting programs. The evidence that dingoes, or whatever you want to call them, play an important role in sustaining healthy, balanced ecosystems is strong, but nowhere in Australia are there any serious moves to conserve them. A key reason for this lack of action is an "identity crisis" brought about by the ambiguous language that has increasingly been adopted to describe them.

Mike Letnic

Correspondence

Stephen Romei

I'm writing this at Easter, when the fresh seafood retailers of Sydney, where I live, are even busier than usual. Their display ice-scapes teem with recent life, and extant life for that matter. As always, I look away from the mud crabs, bound and stacked in their plastic crates. But this year it is the octopuses, tentacles twitching, that I most avoid. The reason? An article in the November/December issue of *Orion* magazine, "Deep Intellect: Inside the Mind of the Octopus," by Sy Montgomery. You can read the piece on the magazine's website, but the subtitle goes to the heart of the matter: octopuses, it seems, have not just brains (and several of them), but *minds*. One example: they remember people, especially people they dislike, a sign of intelligence if ever there was one. Montgomery, who has long had a thing for octopuses, writes about staring at one in a tank and wondering "if she was staring back at me – and if so, what was she thinking?" He continues:

> Not long ago, a question like this would have seemed foolish, if not crazy. How can an octopus *know* anything, much less form an opinion? Octopuses are, after all "only" invertebrates … But now, increasingly, researchers … are convinced these boneless, alien animals … have developed intelligence, emotions and individual personalities. Their findings are challenging our understanding of consciousness itself.

And so now when I look at the octopuses in the seafood store, I think, Are they *thinking*? Are they thinking, "What is happening to me?" And then I consider my purchase – faceless oysters – and wonder if one day I'll have to stop eating them, too.

Animal welfare has become an emotionally charged issue in recent years. There are extremists, indeed outright kooks, on both sides of the debate and there is a lot of wilful ignorance in between. So, in responding to Anna Krien's *Quarterly Essay* it's perhaps best to start with my own feelings on the matter. In short, I believe that all animals are entitled to live their lives, and that we have no right to take those lives from them. I think this of ants and cockroaches and of chimps and dolphins, of the commonest and dumbest and ugliest beasts and the rarest and smartest and cutest creatures. I hate the abuse of the word "humane" to describe less cruel methods of killing animals: I don't know of any living being that does not violently resist its own extinction, except humans.

So, while I think that small-scale organic farming is better than factory farming, I prefer not to eat the output of either process. The most powerful work of animal advocacy I have read is the 2002 book *Dominion: The Power of Man, the Suffering of Animals and the Call to Mercy*, by Matthew Scully, who is, among other things, a former speechwriter to George W. Bush. Scully considers the unassuming lives of animals, so insignificant compared with ours, and writes: "it is the life given to them ... It is all they have. It is their part of the story ... and who is anyone to treat it lightly? Nothing to us – but for them it is the world." And how casually we end these worlds – billions of them a year – "as if their little share of the word's happiness and grief were inconsequential, meaningless, beneath a man's attention." Alice Walker, best known for her 1982 novel *The Colour Purple*, also puts it well: "The animals of the world exist for their own reasons. They were not made for humans any more than black people were made for white, or women created for men." This sort of thinking speaks to me, and so it is that I do my imperfect best not to harm any animal, or be complicit in their harm.

I've been a flawed vegetarian (with frequent lapses into fish) for a decade. I don't buy leather. I'm on the council of the Sydney-based animal welfare group Voiceless. I'm not an animal lover, far from it: in an ideal world I'd have no pets. But I do have dogs and I feed them meat, as I do the children. I love horse racing. So, imperfect indeed, and for that reason I do not judge. One of my best friends is the sort of bloke who orders lamb chops for his entrée and sirloin steak for his main course, and there are few people I'd rather dine with. (He has excellent taste in wine.)

No doubt because of my own struggles, I find Krien's approach to the animal question refreshing. She starts her piece by confessing to doubts as to whether the subject is serious enough for a *Quarterly Essay*. I understand such concerns but think them misplaced. Animal welfare may not be the next great social justice movement, as the Australian lawyer David Weisbrot famously predicted, but certainly it will be one of them. To review Krien's essay for the *Spectator Australia*'s 31 March 2012 issue, I consulted my relatively modest library on the topic: from polemics such as *Dominion* and Peter Singer's landmark 1975 text *Animal Liberation* to questing, self-questioning works such as Michael Pollan's *The Omnivore's Dilemma* and Jonathan Safran Foer's *Eating Animals*, to the burgeoning body of work on the emotional lives of animals, including Jeffrey Moussaieff Masson's *The Pig Who Sang to the Moon* and Irene Pepperberg's *Alex and Me* (about a garrulous parrot). I sense there is an appetite for books such as these, to which we now can add Krien's own intelligently conflicted contribution.

Early in the piece Krien describes her rather typical relationship with animals: she has eaten them, she has worn their skins, she has used products tested on them. At the same time she dismisses as a "farce" any question of whether our treatment of animals is just. "The real question is," she writes, "just how much of this injustice are we prepared to live with?" I agree that is the question. And while this does not diminish Krien's journalistic investigation, I find it surprising that she held both views at the outset, that she bought the "farce." I'd like to know if that has changed – after having visited an Indonesian abattoir, having spent time with hunters, having talked to people who experiment on animals, just how much injustice is she now prepared to live with?

For what it's worth, I ended her essay vowing to redouble my efforts to do less harm. It was her chapter on the Sumatran slaughterhouse, a stand-out piece of reporting, that did it for me. This is why: the abattoir Krien visits is a good one. The Queensland man who runs it has invested heavily in technology and personnel in an attempt to minimise the animals' ordeal. The locals who do the slaughtering are not cruel people (credit to Krien for making this point). All involved are committed to doing the right thing. And yet what happens is none-theless – and here I'll paraphrase Krien's witness statement – fucking horrible.

While it's generally unhelpful to criticise writers for what they didn't write, I will briefly say that Krien's essay all but ignores the great shame of "us and them," which is factory farming: the billions of "them" born into misery, removed from their parents, confined and mistreated for the duration of their brief lives and killed with industrial brutality. Billions every year. It's a system-ised slaughter that has drawn comparisons with the Holocaust, from Isaac Bashevis Singer and, more recently, J.M. Coetzee. (Singer also said, more twinklingly, that he did not become a vegetarian for his health, but for "the health of the chick-ens.") I would include commercial fishing, with its devastating impact on aquatic life and marine habitats, in the broad definition of factory farming. To be fair, it would have been difficult to incorporate so vast and complex an issue into the journalistic format of Krien's piece. Factory farming deserves a *Quarterly Essay* of its own: it's one of those issues long ignored, yet now impossible to ignore. And it affects just about everyone. Safran Foer puts the case well in *Eating Animals*: "Perhaps in the back of our minds we already understand, without all the science I've discussed, that something terribly wrong is happening. Our sustenance now comes from misery."

Of all the stories Krien tells, the one I keep thinking about is Val Plumwood's. In 1985, Plumwood, an environmental activist and feminist intellectual, was on a canoeing trip in Kakadu when a crocodile almost ate her. She wrote about her terrifying, humbling experience – the reptile death-rolled her three times before she managed to escape – in a 2000 essay, "Being Prey." The passage that sticks in my mind is this:

> The thought, *This can't be happening to me, I am a human being, I am more than food!* was one component of my terminal incredulity. It was a shocking reduction, from a complex human being to a mere piece of meat. Reflection has persuaded me that not just humans but any creature can make the same claim to be more than just food.

Plumwood goes on to say she was a vegetarian before the croc attack (and unsurprisingly remained one afterwards), not because predation itself is wrong, but "because I object to the reduction of animal lives in factory farming systems that treat them as living meat." And this brings me to the book that, on my reading at least, is the most remarkable critique of industrial farming yet written. It's a novel, *Under the Skin*, by the Dutch-born, Australian-raised author Michel Faber. Now, spoiler alert, I'm going to give away the plot here, so if you'd rather not know, stop reading and get the book; you won't regret it. For those still with me, here's what happens in Faber's story (well, what I think happens; it's not spelled out): an alien work team on earth is kidnapping humans (men only), bulking them up under typical factory farm conditions, slaughtering them and sending the meat back home for consumption. Here, the big-breasted alien (though, in a neat inversion, the aliens' name for themselves is "human being") who lures the victims (hitchhikers mainly) considers a "vodsel," who, castrated, tongue-docked and fat, is ready for butchering:

> The monthling's eyes were blinking rapidly; a frown was forming on his dome-like forehead. Something was going to happen to him which might be beyond his capacity to stoically endure. He had come to rely on his own bulk, his own indifference to discomfort. Now he sensed he was about to be taken out of his depth.

When you read what happens to the "vodsels," you will be sickened and appalled. You will ask how anyone could treat another being so monstrously. But the "human beings" do not consider themselves monsters. "Vodsels," after all, are just living meat. When I read Faber's book, I was reminded of another novel, written almost a century earlier: Upton Sinclair's 1906 book *The Jungle*. Sinclair's main concern was the lot of immigrant workers in the United States, but his depictions of their toil in the Chicago meatworks show he was attuned to the privations and suffering of another "other." Describing a pork factory in ruthless action – the hogs "so very human in their protests" – he reports that "now and then a visitor wept, to be sure." But, he continues, "this slaughtering machine ran on, visitors or no visitors. It was like some horrible crime scene committed in a dungeon, all unseen and unheeded, buried and out of sight and of memory." Out of sight and out of memory: that remains true to an extent, but it is changing, and fast.

Stephen Romei

James Woodford

Through most of Anna Krien's essay I could feel a knot in my stomach, and it grew tighter and tighter as I tried to rationalise, absorb and understand some of the horrors she detailed. It is easy to say that the worst excesses of animal mistreatment happened in the past (as with the chimp examples that she gave), but I couldn't help feeling the legacy of such cruelty is like an ethical asbestosis, but worse because of the lessons *unlearned*.

However inadequately, at least the asbestos executives of the last half of the twentieth century have been pursued in the courts and found despicable by public opinion. Their victims have been compensated and the entire industry repudiated. On the other hand, those who misused primates and other animals in the name of science, product development and advances in medicine are now in respected retirement. And yet their unpunished, unrepudiated actions from decades (or much less) ago cause horror to contemporary generations.

Like a ruined lung, ethical asbestosis makes our entire society and the structures it is built on look decayed and sick. The terrible moment, the act of cruelty, may be something that we can attribute to a person dead or a time passed, but there is a sense that it comes home to us as a deep moral pain – sometimes decades later. Breathe and accept one particle of such horrible cruelty, use a product derived from such pain, eat food manufactured by such a system, and a moral decay begins.

What may have seemed innocuous at the time, such as sending a chimp into space and releasing photos of his "smile" for the world to "enjoy" before dispatching the creature to a retirement of medical experiments, now seems hideous. At what price do we gain progress? On how many backs is it fair to stand before the cost is too high? Do we want people in our society who have become so blind to the agony of other species that they cease to feel any moral sensibility when treating another creature poorly?

And yet the mistreatment goes on. Perhaps we get better at thinking we can displace onto others the ethical dilemma of how to treat animals. Perhaps direct responsibility can be sheeted home to a poor abattoir worker in the developing world or a science laboratory in a nation where the rules are more lax. But, ultimately, when the knowledge of the misbehaviour is brought out into the sunlight, it is all of us who are diminished. Consciousness is a terrible thing.

It is easy to abhor such straightforward examples as those Krien details, but down to what level can a predatory omnivore such as a human afford to analyse the pain of other creatures? There is so much indirect violence inflicted on animals – from the choice of buying a beautiful deck made of timber from Southeast Asian rainforests, the car that is fuelled by oil mined from a despoiled African nation such as Nigeria, or even the most ethically sound vegetarian food sourced from a paddock that was once wild woodland.

Perhaps the pain of such thinking becomes crippling. Perhaps the morality is about intent. Either way we must take more control of our lives and ask what is acceptable and unacceptable. We must ask questions of everything that our society offers to us in the guise of a material advance. Every step we take away from nature is a step away from moral clarity about the way nature is treated. And, above all, we must look to the future. What are we doing now that will pollute the moral lives of future generations?

James Woodford

Response to
Correspondence

Anna Krien

"So, what are you?" a woman repeatedly asked me after an event for Us and Them, wanting to know if I was vegetarian, vegan or neither. I clamped my mouth shut, although my answer would have pleased her, perhaps even earned a salute. Solutions, answers and, inevitably, an ideology – for the readers of my Quarterly Essay whom I left agitated, I sense this is what they wanted. A position. As James R. Douglas wrote on Meanjin's blog regarding the essay, "on my first read through I was constantly on the prowl for some kind of contention to hang my hat on or ruthlessly demolish."

Us and Them is a very personal essay, and certainly not a platform to promote my daily habits. More importantly, I'm not writing for people who already know what they think, to affirm what they believe or don't believe, or to say what they expect to hear. What I am trying to say in my essay is, "Here are some thoughts, information put in a digestible way – now know your mind, don't handball this."

Other criticisms regarding Us and Them seem to be about what I didn't write. Among the correspondents, B.J. Coman says that I ought to have written about Aldo Leopold's Sand County Almanac in my chapter on hunting; Geoff Russell writes that I focus on small obvious moments, intimacies instead of ratios and vast realities; and Stephen Romei – quite rightly – points out the glaring omission of an in-depth investigation of Australia's factory farming. As Charlotte Wood wrote in a review published in the Australian:

> Only two of this chapter's twenty-four pages deal with the "half-a-billion" animals raised for food (I presume annually) in Australia. The difficulty of omission is familiar to all writers – one simply can't include everything – but to me this brevity is Us and Them's only significant flaw.

A flaw I was, and am, keenly aware of.

All these criticisms seem to me to be more about craft than the issues. Writing is a craft. As when tuning an engine, you have to measure an essay, making sure it doesn't rev too high or too low, that the driver doesn't lurch forward or stop at a standstill on a busy highway. In other words, how to keep the reader reading?

And although eating animals is undoubtedly modern humanity's most significant injustice inflicted on other species, not only in our direct treatment of the "product" but also, as Russell points out, in indirect ramifications such as habitat clearance and overfishing, my essay was not that essay.

As Romei suggests, eating animals deserves its own *Quarterly Essay* – a piece that explores not just the treatment of livestock, bobby calves, battery hens and eternally pregnant and cooped-up sows, or the clearing of bush, trawling of ocean, the effect of hooves on this very ancient continent, but also the unchecked power of supermarkets, the shift from farmer to producer, and, finally, the hedonism of consumers and cheapskates alike. In the same breath, to be all-encompassing one would also then have to explore alternative diets and weigh up whether such solutions bring to the table a new set of difficulties.

Another writer may have been able to accomplish this in a single chapter without their reader feeling completely overwhelmed, but I know my limits. As for writing about Aldo Leopold, again this is an issue of craft – Aldo, although wonderful, has been done to death.

However, Coman's contention that I mistakenly focused on "emoticon" species rather than "general ideas" in the hunting chapter is about more than craft. I sense that the existence of the dingo rattles him. Coman notes that I largely maintain a balanced judgment until I get to the topic of dingoes, which also happens to be a topic dear to him. I wonder if this is a common reaction – do scientists and laboratory researchers think I was totally out of line in the testing chapter, but wonderfully objective in the others? It reminds me of the internal clause I wrote about at the beginning of my essay:

> It seems most of us have a minor clause inside us on the treatment
> of animals – a "that's not allowed" but "that's okay." We have our
> limits and our permissions.

I think it's easier to deal with Coman's criticisms in dot points, at least until we get to the true crux of contention.

1) "In the first instance, she fails to note the difference between hunting pests

and controlling pests. Hunting is a recreational activity that merely harvests pest populations; it does not control them."

This sentence confuses the hell out of me. Instead of writing of "humans," "killing" and "animals," Coman's language is of "recreational activity," "harvest" and "pest populations."

2) "Other means of control are needed and, here again, issues of animal suffering are involved. In fact, they are far more important than those involved in hunting. Compared to myxomatosis, calicivirus and 1080 poison, a minuscule proportion of the rabbit population falls to hunters in Australia."

True, but as Russell points out, I am interested in that eye contact, that physical combat and the attitude that breeds contempt. An issue of craft, I suppose. Plus I wrote about 1080 in my book *Into the Woods* and didn't want to repeat myself.

3) "… all this talk of 'DNA testing' is poppycock."

I agree – but for very different reasons. Perhaps we need to approach the topic in a new way, with the question being not who is native or how long does it take to be a native, but rather, is it part of the ecosystem? Not, is it a pure dingo or a hybrid dingo, but does it *live* like a dingo? Is it constructive or destructive to the ecology of the land? Increasingly, research shows that dingoes are a constructive and elemental part of the ecosystem.

4) "'Oh my god,' she says in an exclamation of surprise, 'this is a total GAME CHANGER' (her emphasis). Well, no, it's not, and that exclamation of surprise is about as convincing in her essay as when you hear it in almost every sentence uttered by teenage schoolgirls.'"

Whatever. (Fiddles with phone.)

5) "Dingo enthusiasts (including some scientists) …"

Coman uses this phrase a couple of times, and I will merely point out that it is loaded and belittling.

6) "The logic for this re-introduction push is that dingoes are a natural part of the ecosystem and help to control introduced vermin animals such as cats and foxes, which prey on small native animals. Unlike 'feral dogs,' they will presumably lay off the sheep, chooks and endangered native mammals because they are more noble."

In all my research, I never had anyone tell me that dingoes would be less likely to attack livestock because they are more "noble." And this is the problem, isn't it? While dingoes may be part of the ecosystem, it is clear that livestock are not. Can the rural and the wild live together?

Here is the crux of the matter. It is not that the dingo is a primitive dog, or a wolf, or that it is a romanticised emoticon, but that it is a threat. An apex predator, to be precise. I'd prefer to have that discussion instead of all this window-dressing.

Guardian dogs are not an easy solution (nor is continued fence maintenance). Maremma sheepdogs and the like require commitment, a fresh take on problem-solving and a concerted effort on behalf of farmers to see their roles anew. It is much easier to push on with aerial baiting and shooting. I am not advocating a point-blank cessation of "pest" control policies, but it is not difficult to smell a rat here.

The purposeful bureaucratic confusion of dingoes and "feral" dogs (which come from where? Farm dogs not desexed? Hunting dogs? Dumped suburban dogs? Whose issue is this really?) seems to imply that there is really only one true concern – that of livestock and efficiency.

But we know the consequences of an unchallenged bounty system and the persecution of a single species. The Tasmanian Tiger was hunted to extinction on the back of myth-mongering and widespread contempt, although it is now clear that the main killers of livestock in Van Diemen's Land were hunting dogs gone feral. Yes, a different animal in a different era, but a similar scenario none-theless. It really wouldn't hurt to apply a policy to the land today that is nuanced and takes into consideration the entire ecology's needs, rather than one of "shoot now, mourn later."

Anna Krien

B.J. Coman was a research scientist with the Victorian Department of Natural Resources for twenty-three years. He is a regular contributor to *Quadrant* and the author of *Tooth and Nail: The Story of the Rabbit in Australia* (1999) and *A Loose Canon* (2007).

Sophie Cunningham is a writer, editor and publisher. Her most recent book is *Melbourne* (2011).

Anna Krien's first book, *Into the Woods* (2010), won the Queensland Premier's Literary Award for Non-Fiction and the Victorian Premier's People's Choice Award. Her writing has been published in the *Monthly*, the *Age*, *Best Australian Essays*, *Best Australian Stories* and the *Big Issue*.

Mike Letnic is an ecologist and Australian Research Council Future Fellow at the University of New South Wales.

Stephen Romei is literary editor of the *Australian*.

Geoff Russell is a mathematician by training, a long-time member of Animal Liberation in South Australia, and the author of *CSIRO Perfidy* (2009).

Thomas Ryan is a social worker, an associate fellow of the Oxford Centre for Animal Ethics, and the author of *Animals and Social Work: A Moral Introduction* (2011).

Laura Tingle is political editor of the *Australian Financial Review*. She won the Paul Lyneham Award for Excellence in Press Gallery Journalism in 2004, and Walkley awards in 2005 and 2011. In 2010 she was shortlisted for the John Button Prize for political writing. She appears regularly on Radio National *Drive* and ABC-TV's *Insiders*.

James Woodford is a science and environment writer and broadcaster. His books include *The Secret Life of Wombats* (2002), winner of the Whitley Award for Best Natural History Book, *The Dog Fence* (2004) and *The Great Barrier Reef* (2010).

SUBSCRIBE to Quarterly Essay & SAVE nearly 40% off the cover price

Subscriptions: Receive a discount and never miss an issue. Mailed direct to your door.
- ☐ **1 year subscription** (4 issues): $49 a year within Australia incl. GST. Outside Australia $79.
- ☐ **2 year subscription** (8 issues): $95 a year within Australia incl. GST. Outside Australia $155.
- * All prices include postage and handling.

Back Issues: (Prices include postage and handling.)

- ☐ **QE 1** ($10.95) Robert Manne *In Denial*
- ☐ **QE 2** ($10.95) John Birmingham *Appeasing Jakarta*
- ☐ **QE 4** ($10.95) Don Watson *Rabbit Syndrome*
- ☐ **QE 5** ($12.95) Mungo MacCallum *Girt by Sea*
- ☐ **QE 6** ($12.95) John Button *Beyond Belief*
- ☐ **QE 7** ($12.95) John Martinkus *Paradise Betrayed*
- ☐ **QE 8** ($12.95) Amanda Lohrey *Groundswell*
- ☐ **QE 10** ($13.95) Gideon Haigh *Bad Company*
- ☐ **QE 11** ($13.95) Germaine Greer *Whitefella Jump Up*
- ☐ **QE 12** ($13.95) David Malouf *Made in England*
- ☐ **QE 13** ($13.95) Robert Manne with David Corlett *Sending Them Home*
- ☐ **QE 14** ($14.95) Paul McGeough *Mission Impossible*
- ☐ **QE 15** ($14.95) Margaret Simons *Latham's World*
- ☐ **QE 16** ($14.95) Raimond Gaita *Breach of Trust*
- ☐ **QE 17** ($14.95) John Hirst *"Kangaroo Court"*
- ☐ **QE 18** ($14.95) Gail Bell *The Worried Well*
- ☐ **QE 19** ($15.95) Judith Brett *Relaxed & Comfortable*
- ☐ **QE 20** ($15.95) John Birmingham *A Time for War*
- ☐ **QE 21** ($15.95) Clive Hamilton *What's Left?*
- ☐ **QE 22** ($15.95) Amanda Lohrey *Voting for Jesus*
- ☐ **QE 23** ($15.95) Inga Clendinnen *The History Question*
- ☐ **QE 24** ($15.95) Robyn Davidson *No Fixed Address*
- ☐ **QE 25** ($15.95) Peter Hartcher *Bipolar Nation*
- ☐ **QE 26** ($15.95) David Marr *His Master's Voice*
- ☐ **QE 27** ($15.95) Ian Lowe *Reaction Time*
- ☐ **QE 28** ($15.95) Judith Brett *Exit Right*
- ☐ **QE 29** ($16.95) Anne Manne *Love & Money*
- ☐ **QE 30** ($16.95) Paul Toohey *Last Drinks*
- ☐ **QE 31** ($16.95) Tim Flannery *Now or Never*
- ☐ **QE 32** ($16.95) Kate Jennings *American Revolution*
- ☐ **QE 33** ($17.95) Guy Pearse *Quarry Vision*
- ☐ **QE 34** ($17.95) Annabel Crabb *Stop at Nothing*
- ☐ **QE 36** ($17.95) Mungo MacCallum *Australian Story*
- ☐ **QE 37** ($20.95) Waleed Aly *What's Right?*
- ☐ **QE 38** ($20.95) David Marr *Power Trip*
- ☐ **QE 39** ($20.95) Hugh White *Power Shift*
- ☐ **QE 41** ($20.95) David Malouf *The Happy Life*
- ☐ **QE 42** ($20.95) Judith Brett *Fair Share*
- ☐ **QE 43** ($20.95) Robert Manne *Bad News*
- ☐ **QE 44** ($20.95) Andrew Charlton *Man-Made World*
- ☐ **QE 45** ($20.95) Anna Krien *Us and Them*

Payment Details: I enclose a cheque/money order made out to Schwartz Media Pty Ltd. Please debit my credit card (Mastercard or Visa accepted).

Card No. ☐☐☐☐ ☐☐☐☐ ☐☐☐☐ ☐☐☐☐

Expiry date /   **Amount $**

Cardholder's name   **Signature**

Name

Address

Email   **Phone**

Post or fax this form to: Quarterly Essay, Reply Paid 79448, Collingwood VIC 3066 / Tel: (03) 9486 0288 / Fax: (03) 9486 0244 / Email: subscribe@blackincbooks.com
Subscribe online at **www.quarterlyessay.com**